HEAVEN and HELL

A Biblical Guide

DR. ROBERT P. LIGHTNER

Dr Lightner is my good friend for nearly 70 yrs. We were fellow Seminary Students & sang in a Quartet together! Read it slowly & carefully, it's the Truth, I love you —

DISPENSATIONAL
PUBLISHING HOUSE, INC.

Earl Lightfoot! Dan Schatt — July 2018

Printed in the United States of America

First Edition, First Printing, 2017

ISBN: 978-1-945774-17-1

Dispensational Publishing House, Inc.
PO Box 3181
Taos, NM 87571

www.dispensationalpublishing.com

Ordering Information:
Quantity sales. Special discounts are available on quantity purchases by churches, associations, and others. For details, contact the publisher at the address above.

Orders by U.S. trade bookstores and wholesalers. Please contact the publisher:
Tel: (844) 321-4202

1 2 3 4 5 6 7 8 9 10

Table of Contents

Introduction...1

Heaven..5
    What About Heaven and the "Heavens?"...............................5
    Who Will Go to Heaven?...6
    Who Cannot Go to Heaven?..7
    What About Those Who Cannot Believe?..................................7
    What Will Heaven Be Like?...26
    Some Biblical Descriptions of Heaven.....................................46
    The Believer's Blessed Hope..47
    Conclusion 49

Hell..51
    Introduction 51
    Some Views of Hell Among Bible Believers.............................52
    Hell in the Old Testament..54
    Hell in the New Testament...55

What About Suicide?...59

What About God's Future Judgments?.....................................63
    The Judgment Seat of Christ..63
    The Great White Throne Judgment..65
    The Judgment of Satan and Wicked Angels............................67

Where Will You Spend Eternity?...69
    God's Plan of Salvation 69
    The Holy Spirit's Role in Salvation 78
    The Human Condition of Salvation..84

What Have We Discovered?...97

Bibliography 101

INTRODUCTION

Things *seem* to be getting worse and worse in our world today. Of course, there always have been different views related to the Bible, the church, politics, education, medicine, etc. However, in our complex, modern-day world, it is not getting easier for us to hold on to the truth that we have been taught. All of us need to have the Bible as our guide in deciding what we should believe and how we should behave.

Where I grew up in Pennsylvania, I heard a lot of people saying, "Heavenly days," "Good heavens," "Hell no," and "What the hell?" Maybe you have heard and still hear people talking in this way. I decided to undertake in-depth study to see what the Bible says about heaven and hell. This book contains the results of my study.

Today, there is an alarming number of those who claim to accept the cardinal doctrines of the Christian faith but do not accept what the Bible says about the eternal punishment of those who have not accepted the Lord Jesus Christ as their personal Savior. Yet, they believe in the eternal bliss for those who go to heaven. That sounds very strange and inconsistent to me, especially since these people do not believe in the eternal punishment of hell. The Bible clearly teaches that all outside of Christ will experience eternal punishment in hell.

I believe everyone faces death and life-after-death either in heaven or hell. There is an eternity for everyone—young, old and older. And according to the Bible, we cannot escape this reality.

Among evangelicals, there is no doubt or debate that time, as we know it, will not go on forever. Eternity is as much a future certainty as time is a present reality.

When will the present time end and eternity begin? How will eternity be ushered in? These questions are answered differently by evangelicals, but they do not dispute the fact that there is a real future world out there. No believing student of the Bible accepts the notion that death ends it all. Evangelicals believe in an eternal existence for man, either in heaven or hell. They also agree that one day there will be a new heaven and a new earth. And they believe these things because the Bible teaches them.

Concerning heaven, Jesus said to His own: "I go to prepare a place for you" (John 14:2). Where He would be, He wanted them also. The historic Christian faith has always held that heaven is a place, not a subjective condition that may be enjoyed now and projected into the future at death. Those rightly related to God through His Son are said to be with Him and within that place, in contrast to those outside of Christ who have no hope. Eternal life is the reward of the righteous (cf. John 3:16; Rom. 2:7), which all the redeemed share alike, but there will also be rewards given commensurate with service rendered on earth by the believer (cf. 1 Cor. 3:11-17).

Hell, Jesus taught, is also a place and not simply a condition. He presented it as a place of eternal torment for the devil, his angels and the sons and daughters of Adam who reject Him and His sacrifice for their sins. It is a place of damnation where "the fire is not quenched" (Mark 9:48; cf. Matt. 23:33). Those who have not received God's forgiveness in

Christ will spend eternity in the place called "the lake of fire" (Rev. 20:10, 14, 15; cf. 19:20).

Berkhof summarizes the Bible's teaching on hell in these words:

> Positively, it may be said to consist in (a) a total absence of the favor of God; (b) an endless disturbance of life as a result of the complete domination of sin; (c) positive pains and sufferings in body and soul; and (d) such subjective punishments as pangs of conscience, anguish, despair, weeping, and gnashing of teeth, Matt. 8:12; 13:50; Mark, 9:43, 44, 47, 48; Lk. 16:23, 27; Rev. 14:10; 21:8. Evidently, there will be degrees in the punishment of the wicked. This follows from such passages as Matt. 11:22, 24; Luke 12:47, 48; 20:17. Their punishment will be commensurate with their sinning against the light which they had received.[1]

Evangelicals also agree that there will be "a new heaven and a new earth" in the future (Rev. 21:1). One part of the Bible that this belief is based on is the prophet Isaiah's recording of Jehovah's answer to the prayer of the believing remnant:

> "For, behold, I create new heavens and a new earth: and the former shall not be remembered, nor come into mind". (Isa. 65:17)

Isaiah also records this in Isaiah 66:22:

> "For as the new heavens, and the new earth, which I will make, shall remain before me, saith the LORD, so shall your seed and your name remain."

In New Testament times, Peter was still predicting judgment upon:

> ... heavens and the earth which are now. ... the heavens shall pass away with a great noise, and the elements shall melt with fervent heat, the earth also and the works that are therein shall be burned up" (2 Peter 3:7,10).

---

1 Louis Berkhof, *Systematic Theology* (Grand Rapids; Eerdmans, 1968), p. 736.

But he prophesied even further:

> "We . . . look for new heavens and a new earth, wherein dwelleth righteousness" (2 Pet. 3:13)

John, in his apocalyptic vision, saw Christ on a throne, and "from (His) face the earth and the heaven fled away" (Rev. 20:11).

The present heavens and earth have not yet been destroyed. This prophecy awaits future fulfillment, and so does the prophecy of the creation of a new heaven and earth. Evangelicals do not differ on these things. They agree that the eternal state has not yet begun.

Evangelicals have much in common in the area of eschatology. They agree on the basic essentials of God's plan for the future. And yet evangelicals do differ on many of the specifics related to unfulfilled prophecy.

The battle over the future did not just begin; it has been waged for a long, long time. If anything, the conflict seems to be getting worse rather than better, both from the standpoint of its intensity and the kinds of weapons being used in the battle. Sides are often taken without a thorough understanding of the position or its subsequent effect on other doctrinal beliefs.

We need to be doubly sure our motives and attitudes are pure in approaching this subject. If ever there was a time when we needed to manifest the fruit of the Spirit and every Christian grace, it is in the study of future things. Always we must remember that we are dealing with other members of the body of Christ, fellow members of the household of faith, fellow citizens of the kingdom of God's dear Son.

As a committed premillennialist who also embraces the pretribulational dispensational viewpoint, I will make every effort to heed the above in the discussion that follows.

HEAVEN

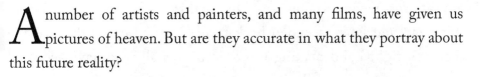

A number of artists and painters, and many films, have given us pictures of heaven. But are they accurate in what they portray about this future reality?

WHAT ABOUT HEAVEN AND THE "HEAVENS?"

The terms "heaven" and "heavens" have been used in different ways throughout the Bible. For example, Abraham stated,

> Lord GOD, what wilt thou give me, seeing I go childless, and the steward of my house *is* this Eliezer of Damascus? And Abram said, Behold, to me thou hast given no seed: and, lo, one born in my house is mine heir. And, behold, the word of the LORD *came* unto him, saying, This shall not be thine heir; but he that shall come forth out of thine own bowels shall be thine heir. And he brought him forth abroad, and said, Look now toward heaven, and tell the stars, if thou be able to number them: and he said unto him, So shall thy seed be. (Gen. 15:2-5)

A large number of other texts used the plural "heavens" as well (see, for example, Gen. 19:24; 1 Kings 8:23 and Eccles. 1:13).

WHO WILL GO TO HEAVEN?

All who have accepted the Lord Jesus Christ as their personal Savior will be eternal occupants of heaven. And all who as infants could not believe will be there also. I will give a defense of this truth later in this book.

Heaven is the place where God dwells now. Imagine that for a moment: God the Son and God the Holy Spirit are there also.

When Jesus was here on earth, He taught about heaven. All four of His gospels—Matthew, Mark, Luke and John—record His teaching. He has given us proof that He, the Lord Jesus Christ, died on the cross paying for our sins. On the third day, He was raised from the dead and later ascended back to heaven and currently is at the Father's right hand making intercession for all who have accepted Him as their personal Savior.

Luke tells us about Christ's ascension back to heaven in these words:

> And he led them out as far as to Bethany, and he lifted up his hands, and blessed them. And it came to pass, while he blessed them, he was parted from them, and carried up into heaven. And they worshipped Him, and returned to Jerusalem with great joy. (Luke 24:50-52)

And again in Acts 1:8, Luke describes Christ's ascension back to heaven. In this verse, Luke writes that after Christ gathered His disciples together, minus Judas Iscariot, He told them they would receive power when the Holy Spirit came upon them and they were to be His witnesses throughout their world. "And when he had spoken these things, while they beheld, he was taken up; and a cloud received Him out of their sight" (Acts 1:9).

WHO CANNOT GO TO HEAVEN?

I suspect that most people who believe there is a heaven hope they will go there when they die. Most people who believe there is such a place as hell would most likely definitely assert they do not want to go there. The question before us is, who, in fact, will go to hell? The answer according to the Bible is that all who have not accepted the Lord Jesus Christ as their personal Savior will go to hell after death.

That does not make me, or any others I know, glad. Neither does God delight in the fact that hell is real and sure and that those who reject His Son will go there for all eternity. Nowhere in the Bible are we told that God chose some people to go to hell. However, it does tell us that "For God so loved the world, that he gave His only begotten Son, that whosoever believeth in Him should not perish, but have everlasting life. For God sent not His Son into the world to condemn the world; but that the world through Him might be saved" (John 3:16-17). It has always been true that all who do not accept Christ as their Savior will be lost forever; but, God has provided salvation from hell through His Son.

WHAT ABOUT THOSE WHO CANNOT BELIEVE?

Every human being is born in sin. In Romans, we are told that "all have sinned, and come short of the glory of God" (Rom. 3:23) and that, "There is none righteous, no, not one" (Rom. 3:10). In Ephesians, Paul writes that all are "children of wrath" at birth (Eph. 2:3).

The Lord Jesus Christ has made provision for the salvation of everyone in His substitutionary death. Every member of Adam's race is redeemable. However, there is only one way of salvation. The sinner can only be justified or declared righteous before God through the finished work of Christ. The only way of salvation is through Christ and His finished work. His death in the stead of every person is the basis of salvation; it is the only ground upon which God can forgive sin. And what is more, only one condition of salvation is set forth in the Bible—the Lord Jesus Christ must be accepted by faith. He must be received as personal Savior; and when He is received, His completed work of salvation is applied to the believer.

But what happens to all those who cannot meet this one condition of salvation due to mental incapability? I believe firmly that all such receive eternal life. When they die, they go to heaven. No one will spend eternity in the eternal punishment of hell who was not able to believe, to meet God's one condition of salvation. This conviction will now be defended—first, from several general Biblical considerations and then from the study of specific passages of Scripture.

Several facts of Scripture not only relate to the question of salvation for those who cannot believe but, in fact, support the contention that all who cannot believe will not be eternally doomed. Some of these provide a stronger argument than others. Taken together–and they must be to get the whole picture—they constitute formidable evidence. No particular significance is attached to the order in which they are presented here.

Children in the Bible. Many, many times the words *children* and *child* appear in the Bible. Both the Old and New Testaments abound with these words. From these many references, we may be sure that little ones have a definite place in the great heart of God and in His sovereign plan.

Not once in all the references to infants is there so much as a hint that they will ever be damned to eternal perdition after death, should they die before they have opportunity to respond to the gospel. In many contexts where the words are used, we would not expect a statement about the individual's eternal destiny. Yet there are instances, such as when God ordered the destruction of all the Amalekites—including infants (1 Sam. 15:3) —when it would have been most appropriate. But not once, even when reference is made to the death of children, is there so much as a hint that any would suffer eternal separation from God (see, for example, Ex. 12:29- 30 and Matt. 2:16).

Why, we ask reverently, are we not told that those who cannot respond in faith to Christ spend eternity with those who reject the Savior if, in fact, they do? Those who cannot believe are not told in the Bible to believe nor are they expected to do so. They are not classified as wicked evildoers and rejecters of God's grace. It is always adults who are addressed, either directly or indirectly, with regard to these matters. Since the Bible has so much to say about those who cannot believe and yet says nothing about their eternal separation from God because of their inability, we may conclude that they have heaven as their home.

The Person of God. A number of the descriptive characteristics of God found in the Bible lend strong support to our contention: There is salvation for all those who cannot respond to the gospel. They are safe in heaven's bliss after death. These truths also provide comfort for the bereaved.

The characteristics or attributes of God tell us much more than what He does or how He acts. They are not qualities which are simply attached to His Person nor are they simply actions that He does. He actually *is* each of these things. They are His essence. They describe His Person, not merely His behavior.

Without imposing human ideas on these Divine characteristics, it would seem incongruous with the very nature of God if any who cannot believe die and go to hell. Consider His attributes with this in mind.

God's Wisdom. God has made no mistakes, and He never will make one. In wisdom, He has chosen and implemented the plan of redemption which will bring the most glory to Himself. His Son is the Savior Who died for all. Wisely, God has prescribed one way of salvation and only one. Apart from the Lord Jesus Christ, His Son, there is no salvation. Those who reject Him as their personal Savior are forever lost. They have no hope and are doomed to eternal damnation.

But those who cannot believe do not refuse God's offer; they do not reject Christ the Savior or God's revelation in nature and human conscience. In infinite wisdom, God cares for them. Since rejection of the Savior is the final reason why men go to hell, those who do not reject Him because they are unable to make a conscious decision enter heaven on the basis of the finished work of Christ. God's plan is a wise plan of redemption because He is wise. It is unthinkable, therefore, to suppose that He assigns to perdition any of those who never had an opportunity either to receive or reject the Redeemer.

God's Love. "God is love" is the clear revelation of Scripture (1 John 4:16). A more tremendous utterance cannot be found in all the Bible. God not only loves, He is love. It seems totally out of harmony with this truth to believe that God would send to the lake of fire any who have not reached a level of mental competence enabling them to decide for the Savior. After all, God did send His Son to die for all. He loved the world enough to do that. Does that love not avail for that same company of people until such a time that it is rejected and spurned? God's infinite love for all is illustrated, supported and strengthened when we see how, in love, He secures the salvation of that large company who cannot believe.

God's Mercy and Grace. The psalmist wrote, "The LORD is merciful and gracious, slow to anger, and plenteous in mercy" (Ps. 103:8). Mercy and grace may be viewed as two sides of one truth. God's mercy means that deserved penalty and punishment are withheld. The grace of God refers to His giving favor to those who do not deserve it.

How do these two perfections of God relate to the question under consideration? They relate in this way: Both God's mercy and His grace were shown at Calvary toward all—those who can and do believe as well as those who can never believe. The punishment for sin, which every member of the human race deserves, was borne by Christ. What we deserved, He received. He cannot be more merciful. What He does for man in salvation is based upon the mercy He revealed at Calvary. God's grace was displayed on that mount, too. There, through the death of His Son, God made it possible to show favor, to save all even though not one deserves it. How, we must ask, could it possibly be said that God was merciful and gracious toward those who cannot believe if, in fact, any of that group perish?

God's Goodness. "The Lord is good" (Nah. 1:7). Does God do good things? Does He do only good things? To both of these questions the answer must be an unqualified *yes.* But could that honestly be said in response to either one of the questions if He damned forever even one who could not meet the requirement for salvation which He Himself set forth?

We do not believe Biblical truth because we can find no objections to it. God calls upon us to believe His Word regardless of the problems it may create for us. The Bible does not teach the damnation of those who cannot believe. It does, instead, teach the goodness of God. It is highly inconsistent with His goodness to believe any who die who cannot believe are doomed. Rather, I believe all such receive eternal life since Scripture nowhere teaches the contrary and since such belief is in perfect accord with God's Person.

God's Justice. "The just Lord," said Zephaniah the prophet, "*is* in the midst thereof [of His people]" (Zeph. 3:5). David the psalmist expressed the same truth regarding God's justice when he said, "The Lord executeth righteousness and judgment for all that are oppressed" (Ps. 103:6).

Since God is just, we may be assured that He deals equitably and according to truth with all His creatures. He is never unfair. But if He demanded of any of His creatures something which they could not do, would He be just? Since God has made it clear in His Word that those who reject His Son as Savior will be damned, how would He be just in refusing into His presence those who were never able to receive or reject His salvation? The Son of God came declaring God's righteousness "that he might be just, and the justifier of him which believeth in Jesus" (Rom. 3:26).

But there are many who cannot believe. What will happen to these? Based upon God's justice and the satisfaction of His offended righteousness because of the work of His Son, we believe He is the *justifier* of those who cannot believe just as certainly as He is of those who can and do believe.

God's Holiness. "God *is* holy" (Ps. 99:9). In 1 John, we are told that "God is light, and in Him is no darkness at all" (1 John 1:5). What about the absolute holiness of God in relation to salvation for those who cannot believe? Since God is holy and since those who cannot believe are born in sin, does it not follow that they cannot be saved? No, it does not!

But it would most certainly be true that those who cannot believe could not receive eternal life if Christ had not died for them and paid for their sin. He did pay the full price demanded by God, because of His offended righteousness, for all men—those who cannot believe as well as those who can believe. No one is condemned to eternal torment in hell, therefore, only because he sinned in Adam and was born in sin. God has done something about that sin and the guilt which resulted from it. The final and ultimate reason for eternal separation from the presence of God is the rejection of His Son as Savior. There is no other way to explain the many passages of Scripture which present faith as the one condition of salvation.

God's Wrath. The Bible has a good deal to say about the wrath of God. However, it is not popular or appealing to talk of this truth about God. Even those who believe in the wrath of God tend to say little about it.

God's wrath must not be understood as His loss of self-control. It is not an outburst of irrational behavior as it is with humanity. Always, those who experience God's wrath receive exactly what they deserve. We can understand the wrath of God by contrasting it with His love. God's love is the expression of an emotional attitude. In the same way, His wrath is just as much the expression of an emotional attitude. It is also an expression of His justice. The contrast between the two is that the former results in His favor (grace) toward the sinner. The latter ends in His punishment of the sinner. God's wrath is displayed toward those who spurn His love.

How does the Biblical teaching about God's wrath relate to the salvation of those who cannot believe? It relates very definitely since those who experience God's wrath deserve it. They enter into it because they refuse God's way of escape from it. Those who cannot believe have not refused God's grace. Do they deserve God's wrath? J. I. Packer summarized the Biblical teaching on God's wrath this way:

> . . . God's wrath in the Bible is something which men choose for themselves. Before hell is an experience inflicted by God, it is a state for which man himself opts, by retreating from the light which God shines in his heart to lead him to Himself. When John writes, 'he who does not believe (in Jesus) is condemned (judged) already, because he has not believed in the name of the only Son of God,' he goes on to explain himself as follows, 'And this is the judgment, that the light has come into the world, and men loved darkness rather than light, because their deeds were evil' (John 3:18f, RSV). He means just what he says: the decisive act of judgment upon the lost is the judgment which they pass upon themselves, by rejecting the light that comes to them in and through Jesus Christ. In the last analysis, all that God does subsequently in judicial action towards the unbeliever, whether in this life or beyond it, is to show him, and lead him into, the full implications of the choice he has made. . . .
>
> We need, therefore to remember that the key to interpreting the many biblical passages, often highly figurative, which picture the divine King and Judge as active against men in wrath and vengeance, is to realize that what God is hereby doing is no more than to ratify and confirm judgments which those whom He "visits" have already passed on themselves by the course they have chosen to follow. This appears in the story of God's first act of wrath towards man, in Genesis 3, where we learn that Adam had already chosen to hide from God, and keep clear of His presence, before ever God drove him from the garden; and the same principle applies throughout the Bible."[2]

---

2 J. I. Packer, *Knowing God* (Downers Grove, IL: InterVarsity Press, 1973), pp. 138-39.

Salvation from God's terrible wrath is found in Christ alone. It is the blood of Christ which appeases God's wrath (Rom. 5:9). Christ's work of propitiation, His sacrifice which satisfied God the Father, averts His wrath. Only upon "his enemies" is God's wrath poured out (Nah. 1:2). Those who cannot believe are not God's enemies. Provisionally, they have been "reconciled to God" (Rom. 5:10).

Surely the eternal torment of hell is a manifestation of God's wrath. Those who will experience the wrath of God in that place will do so because they rejected His love in Christ and thus deserve the consequences. Those who cannot believe cannot disbelieve either and, therefore, we may be sure that they will spend eternity in heaven, not hell.

It is true that all are born in a state of condemnation. That condemnation is removed when people respond to God's provision of grace in Christ. The Bible says,

> He that believeth on Him is not condemned: but he that believeth not is condemned already, because he hath not believed in the name of the only begotten Son of God (John 3:18).

Once more, we come back to the problem which has been coming up again and again: What of those who cannot believe? My answer is, since the price has been paid in full, until it is rejected, the debt is cancelled. Therefore, God can receive into His presence all those who did not receive His Son by faith because they could not do so. Without violating His righteous demands in any way, these are accepted into His presence. After all, His righteous demands were met at Calvary. The debt has been paid! Jesus paid it all! Nothing more is owed to God.

Those who can and do believe do not contribute anything toward the debt of sin by their faith. God's requirement of faith from man is never viewed in Scripture as part of the payment toward man's debt. The debt of sin is only charged against those who reject the payment God the Son has made and God the Father has accepted. All those who cannot believe owe nothing more to God. Those who can believe but do not believe owe the full debt; that is why they cannot go to heaven. Their debt can never be paid by man. To refuse Christ's payment is to seal one's eternal destiny, but to be unable to receive it is to be covered by the payment already made and accepted by God.

Christ's Life and Death. During His earthly ministry, the Lord Jesus gave much attention to children. Benjamin B. Warfield, a great evangelical spokesman of the past, summarized well the Savior's interest in and ministry for children:

> What Jesus did for children, we may perhaps sum up as follows. He illustrated the ideal of childhood in his own life as a child. He manifested the tenderness of his affection for children by conferring blessings upon them in every stage of their development as he was occasionally brought into contact with them. He asserted for children a recognized place in His kingdom, and dealt faithfully and lovingly with each age as it presented itself to him in the course of his work. He chose the condition of childhood as a type of the fundamental character of the recipients of the kingdom of God. He adopted the relation of childhood as the most vivid earthly image of the revelation of God's people to him who was not ashamed to be called their Father which is in heaven, and thus reflected back upon this relation a glory by which it has been transfigured ever since."[3]

What does all of Christ's interest in and ministry for infants and young children mean with regard to the major question within this study? It has much to do with it. Since Christ was so interested in so many who could not believe and since He did so much for them during His life, we have reason to believe He loves all such and grants them eternal life when they die.

---

3 John E. Meeter, ed., *Selected Shorter Writings of Benjamin B Warfield* (Nutley, NJ: Presbyterian and Reformed Publishing Co., 1970), 1:224.

The substitutionary death of Christ also provides support for believing that those who cannot believe are saved at the time of their death. Jesus did die for all. Surely those who cannot believe were not excluded from His gracious provision. No Scripture could be used to defend such a view. As we noted earlier, Christ's death paid the full price for the creature's sin. Until the Savior and His finished work are rejected, therefore, the debt remains cancelled.

Another factor related to Christ's death supports our thesis: If those who cannot believe are not beneficiaries of God's salvation, Christ died for them in vain. Nothing whatsoever was accomplished by His work for them if they are not saved by it. Someone might say, "But what about those who reject Christ's salvation? Of what value or to what avail was His death for them?" The answer is, Christ's death is the basis for the condemnation of such. But surely His death cannot be the basis of the condemnation of those who cannot believe since they could not and did not reject it. Scripture clearly teaches that one who does not believe is condemned for that very reason: "he hath not believed in the name of the only begotten Son of God" (John 3:18).

God's wrath is upon those who believe not:

> "He that believeth on the Son hath everlasting life: and he that believeth not the Son shall not see life; but the wrath of God abideth on him" (John 3:36).

Only if those who cannot believe are saved does the finished work of Christ have any relation whatsoever to them.

The Basis of Judgment for the Lost. The Apostle John saw in his vision "a great white throne" (Rev. 20:11). God was seated on the throne. The dead who appeared before the throne were the unsaved dead since the saved dead had already been raised (v. 5). All the unsaved dead of all the ages were brought to appear before the almighty God. Each one was "judged out of those things which were written in the books, according to their works" (v. 12). All who appeared for this judgment were "cast into the lake of fire," because their names were not "written in the book of life" (v. 15). The reason their names were not *in the book of life* was because they had not believed; they had not received the Lord Jesus Christ as their personal Savior from sin. Their works demonstrated their lost condition.

In a future day, all who are unregenerate and who will spend eternity in the lake of fire will first stand before God at the great white throne judgment. We can be sure that those who died without ever being able to believe will not be there. But how can we be so sure of that? They have no works, having done neither good nor evil. Clearly, the basis of judgment at this future time of judgment will be according to what those being judged have done. Equally as clear, all the unsaved will appear there. Since those who died before they could believe have no works, we may be sure that they will not appear before the great white throne. And since all the unsaved will most certainly appear there, we may also be sure that those who cannot believe are not unsaved. If they are not among the unregenerate and will not appear before God at this time, we can conclude happily that they are among the redeemed. There most certainly is salvation for those who cannot believe! They all do go to heaven, not hell.

The Merit of Faith. No serious student of Scripture doubts the necessity of personal faith for salvation on the part of those who can exercise it. But why do people exercise faith in Christ? What motivates them to do it? Do they simply decide on their own without any influence outside themselves? No. According to the Bible, the Holy Spirit of God has a very vital part in bringing the sinner to see his need of the Savior and in enabling him to receive Him as his own. In fact, apart from this work of the Holy Spirit, no one would ever believe the gospel and receive Christ as Savior. God the Holy Spirit moves upon the stubborn will of man, enabling him to respond in faith to God's offer of salvation. Jesus spoke of this Divine work upon the human heart when He said,

> No man can come to me, except the Father which hath sent me draw him: and I will raise him up at the last day (John 6:44).

Nowhere in Scripture are we told man is lost because the Spirit of God did not move upon his will. Condemnation is always given because of man's sin and his stubborn rebellion against God, which is climaxed in the rejection of God's Son as Savior.

The Father draws men to Himself as the Spirit of God uses the Word of God to convict of sin and eventually to bring life to the believing sinner (John 3:5; 1 Pet. 1:23). But this ministry of the Spirit is surely not operative upon those who are not able to understand the Word and to respond to the claims of Christ.

Faith has no merit of its own. It adds nothing to the complete salvation provided by Christ. It is not a work. The stalwart soldier against liberalism, J. Gresham Machen, said, "Faith consists not in doing something but in receiving something."[4] And J.I. Packer, similar in thought to Machen, said, "Faith is no more than an activity of reception contributing nothing to that which it receives."[5] The salvation God offers the sinner is an undeserved and completely unearned grace-salvation and is always viewed as a gift in the Bible (see Eph. 2:8- 9).

So the reader may agree, faith has no merit of its own. But what does that have to do with the question at hand? How does this fact relate to the question of the salvation of those who cannot believe? Ah, it has much to do with it, and it is this: Since faith contributed nothing, its absence in those who cannot exercise it does not hinder the sovereign God from accomplishing in them all that He does in those who can and do believe. All who can believe must do so to receive eternal life. All who cannot believe receive the same eternal life provided by Christ for them since they are not

---

4 J. Gresham Machen, *What Is Faith?* (Grand Rapids: Wm. B. Eerdmans Publishing Co., 1925), p. 172.

5 J. I Packer, *Fundamentalism and the Word of God* (Grand Rapids: Wm. B. Eerdmans Publishing Co., 1960), p. 172.

able either to receive or reject it. Freely, God gives life everlasting to all in both groups. Freely He justifies, not in payment of anything owed to the sinner (Rom. 3:24). Since He can justify freely those who believe, He can do the same for those who cannot believe.

Twice in the book of Revelation, John wrote about the redeemed in heaven coming "of all nations, and kindreds, and people, and tongues" (Rev. 7:9; cf. 5:9). The death of so many from the beginning of time who have never reached the decision-making status may be God's way of populating heaven in fulfillment of these Scriptures. It is true that He could, if He so chose, fulfill His Word in some other way. Yet the fact remains that many of the innumerable multitudes which John saw coming from all these quarters may very well be those who were never able to believe.

We have presented support for the belief that all who die without ever being able to believe will spend eternity with God in heaven. Our support came from general Biblical considerations which relate in some way to the question proposed by the thesis of this section. We want to look at some specific passages of Scripture which bear upon the question. Admittedly, not much Scripture deals directly with the subject, but in these pages we will set forth passages which do bolster the view. Not one verse of Scripture which relates in any way to the question at hand can be legitimately used to suggest the view that any of those who died without being able to respond to the Savior are doomed to eternity in hell. The information that God has been pleased to give us provides great and precious promise of eternal salvation for all who cannot believe.

2 Samuel 12:22-23: "And he said, While the child was yet alive, I fasted and wept: for I said, Who can tell *whether* GOD will be gracious to me, that the child may live? But now he is dead, wherefore should I fast? can I bring him back again? I shall go to him, but he shall not return to me."

David, the man after God's own heart, had sinned grievously. He was guilty of adultery and homicide. According to the law, he deserved death! But because he honestly acknowledged his sin, confessed it and did not harden his heart against the Lord, the just penalty was not executed against him.

Because of David's sin, the enemies of the people of God—who were also the enemies of God Himself—blasphemed Israel's God. Shame and reproach were brought upon God and His people. A man's sin always seems to have a way of affecting many others. In the same way, God's honor and justice had to be displayed before His enemies. That is why "the LORD struck the child that Uriah's wife bare unto David, and it was very sick" (2 Sam. 12:15).

David was brought to his senses by the Word of God through the prophet Nathan. The task that God gave to Nathan was a difficult one indeed. Once David was alone, he poured out his heart to God and prayed that the child would be restored. But his request was not granted. "On the seventh day . . . the child died" (2 Sam. 12:18). The servants debated what to do. They gathered to plan their strategy. David saw them, heard them whisper and supposed rightly that the child had died. He then stopped fasting and praying; he "washed, and anointed *himself* . . . and worshipped" the Lord (vv. 19, 20). The servants could not understand his sudden change of behavior. They asked him about it. David's reply constitutes one of the great texts of Scripture in support of the salvation of those not capable of believing (cf. vv. 22, 23).

Life after death was a certainty for David. He firmly believed that he would be with his son again in the future. The psalmist never doubted this for a moment. David was rightly related to Jehovah, and he had no doubt that he would spend eternity with Him. Neither did he have any doubt that his infant son, taken in death before he could decide for or against his father's God, would be there also.

Some argue that David's declaration merely meant he would one day join his son in death. As the child had died, so would the father in due time. But such a view does not account for the anticipated reunion and fellowship with his son which are strongly implied in the statement.

Furthermore, in context, David's act of worship in the house of the Lord is hardly explained if the death of his son is simply a reminder to David of his own certain death.

This weak explanation also fails to account for the contrasting attitude which David had when his son Absalom died. After he became a man, Absalom rebelled against God and sinned terribly. He even attempted to seize his father's kingdom. In one such attempt, he was killed in battle. When David heard of his son's death, he was grief-stricken. He wept bitterly. In fact, he even wished he could have died for his son (2 Sam. 18:33).

Apparently, David was not at all certain of Absalom's salvation and, therefore, of his future; thus, David grieved and wept. But he was sure of the destiny of his infant son. So sure was David of the child's eternal home that he knew he would go to be with him. This assurance caused him to turn from grief to worshipful prayer.

> It was this thought of reunion with his dead child which cheered David; but where did he think the reunion would be? In the grave? In hell? In heaven? He believed that he himself would go to heaven after death and consequently meant to express the belief that his child had but gone on before him to that blessed abode. The idea of meeting his child in the unconscious grave could not have rationally comforted him; nor could the thought of meeting him in hell have cheered his spirit; but the thought of meeting him in heaven had in itself the power of turning his weeping into joy."[6]

Still, others who do believe David was acknowledging the presence of his child in heaven argue that the child was there because he was a child of the covenant. Those who embrace this view believe only the infants who have regenerate parents and who have received infant baptism (the New Testament sign of the covenant, they say) will go to heaven if they die.

Matthew 18:1-14 states:

---

6 R. A. Webb, *The Theology of Infant Salvation* (Clarksville, TN: Presbyterian Committee of Publication, 1907), pp. 20, 21.

"At the same time came the disciples unto Jesus, saying, Who is the greatest in the kingdom of heaven? And Jesus called a little child unto Him, and set him in the midst of them, And said, Verily I say unto you, Except ye be converted, and become as little children, ye shall not enter into the kingdom of heaven. Whosoever therefore shall humble himself as this little child, the same is greatest in the kingdom of heaven. And whoso shall receive one such little child in my name receiveth me. But whoso shall offend one of these little ones which believe in me, it were better for him that a millstone were hanged about his neck, and that he were drowned in the depth of the sea. Woe unto the world because of offences! for it must needs be that offences come; but woe to that man by whom the offence cometh! Wherefore if thy hand or thy foot offend thee, cut them off, and cast them from thee: it is better for thee to enter into life halt or maimed, rather than having two hands or two feet to be cast into everlasting fire. And if thine eye offend thee, pluck it out, and cast it from thee: it is better for thee to enter into life with one eye, rather than having two eyes to be cast into hell fire. Take heed that ye despise not one of these little ones; for I say unto you, That in heaven their angels do always behold the face of my Father which is in heaven. For the Son of man is come to save that which was lost. How think ye? if a man have an hundred sheep, and one of them be gone astray, doth he not leave the ninety and nine, and goeth into the mountains, and seeketh that which is gone astray? And if so be that he find it, verily I say unto you, he rejoiceth more of that sheep, than of the ninety and nine which went not astray. Even so it is not the will of your Father which is in heaven, that one of these little ones should perish." (Matthew 18:1–14) .

Jesus and His disciples returned to Capernaum where He performed a miracle, making it possible to pay the temple tax (cf. Matt. 17:24-27). The very same day, He also settled a dispute among His disciples. They argued on the road from Galilee to Capernaum about who among them would be greatest in the Kingdom (Matt. 18:1; see also Mark 9:33-50; Luke 9:46-50). By *kingdom of heaven* Matthew no doubt meant the earthly Davidic kingdom which Jesus announced and which His disciples expected Him to inaugurate.

To illustrate the need for simple trust and utter dependence, Jesus used a little child. Mark tells us that He even took the little one up "in His arms" (Mark 9:36). This fact helps us understand the approximate age of the child. It was not a tiny infant but was certainly a very young child, or else He would not have taken him in His arms. This was a tender scene indeed. Without pride or resistance, the child allowed the Savior to do this. Those who would enter the kingdom, Jesus said, must have the same attitude toward and dependence upon Him. In fact, no one will ever enter the kingdom who does not become as a little child, said the Savior.

Who will be greatest in the kingdom of heaven? He who humbles himself and has a childlike spirit of trust; it is he who is the greatest (Matt. 18:4). All who *receive* a little child such as Jesus held in His arms will receive Him (v. 5).

Without dispute, Jesus put a high value upon little children. A person's view of his eternal destiny must certainly take this into account. Jesus had the *little child* (v. 2) *in His arms* (Mark 9:36) as He spoke to the disciples. All that He said on this occasion must, therefore, be understood in that light.

For very young children, the tender and receptive spirit which they have toward Jesus is viewed as equivalent to faith in Him. Both Matthew and Mark tell us that Jesus said these little ones "believe in me" (Matt 18:6; Mark 9:42). It is doubtful that the "little ones" referred to were old enough to make a conscious decision for Christ as their personal Savior. Could it be because the little ones did not oppose the Savior, but instead allowed Him to welcome and care for them, that He viewed their lack of rejection as a reception of Him and belief in Him? That seems to have been the case.

Some believe Jesus' words about receiving a child excludes literal children altogether. This would mean His warnings about offending "one of these little ones which believe in me" (Matt. 18:6) and despising "one of these little ones" (v. 10) referred not to little children like the one in His arms but only to those with a childlike spirit—children of the kingdom. The same would be true of the declaration that "it is not the will of your Father which is in heaven, that one of these little ones should perish" (v. 14). Such a view does not place enough significance either upon the physical act of Jesus in this passage or upon what He said with reference to that act.

It seems better to see Jesus as having in mind both actual children, like the one in His arms, and believers, children of the kingdom who become as children in their faith and trust. In other words, Jesus was talking about both literal and spiritual children. He, in fact, equated them in the things He discussed. The reason "these little ones" are not to be made to sin (v. 6) or to be looked down on (v. 10) is because they so represent Jesus that to mistreat them was like mistreating Him.

Every child and every one with a childlike spirit is precious in the sight of Jesus. That is why it is so wrong to despise, to belittle or to neglect one of these. All who are in God's family are very important to Him—those who cannot make a conscious decision and those who exercise childlike trust.

The reason why "one of these little ones" (v. 6) should not be despised is because Jesus said, "That in heaven their angels do always behold the face of my Father" (v. 10). Some believe each child and each Christian has a specific angel assigned to him or her. Others believe holy angels perform a general ministry on behalf of God's children. What is so important about this text of Scripture with respect to our subject is its clear statement that under Divine guidance holy angels do perform a ministry on behalf of *these little ones*. The angels do represent children before God. This truth lends strong support to the fact of their salvation. If both literal young children and children of the kingdom are in view, what is true of the one group is also true of the other.

Another interpretation of Christ's reference to the angels of children is that *their angels* may be the spirits of the little children who had passed from this life. The word *angel* seems to be used this way in Acts 12:15.

Peter was miraculously delivered from prison and appeared at the house of John Mark's mother. A prayer meeting was in process. Rhoda, the aid, answered the knock on the door and, to her complete surprise, found Peter standing there. When she told those who prayed that their prayer had been answered, they could not believe it. They said it could not be Peter but that it was his angel. By this they surely meant, "It is his departed spirit." Since no other Scripture teaches about so-called guardian angels beyond these two instances, some believe the Acts 12:15 usage of *angel* throws light upon Christ's reference to the *angels* of the little ones.

Just as a good shepherd is concerned with all of his sheep and does everything in his power to rescue even one which goes astray, God is vitally concerned with all His own (Matt. 18:12, 13). The shepherd does not want to lose any of his sheep. Jesus said it is that way with His Heavenly Father: "Even so it is not the will of your Father which is in heaven, that one of these little ones should perish" (Matt. 18:14).

Just as the shepherd in Jesus' illustration could not let his wandering sheep perish, so the eternal God in heaven would not and did not will that one of His little ones should perish. When Jesus said this, He was still taking about little children like the one in His arms. Any idea of reprobation for any one of the little children is excluded. For even one who dies without being able to believe, to be lost would be contrary to the Father's will.

Putting it positively, Jesus' statement means none of the little ones ever perish. Indeed, there is salvation for all who die before they can choose to follow Christ as Savior.

WHAT WILL HEAVEN BE LIKE?

The Blessed Hope

The Apostle Paul called heaven a "blessed hope" (Tit. 2:13). This hope is not just something believers wish to happen. Rather, believers have the hope and certainty of heaven because they are related to the Lord Jesus Christ. This relationship is what makes it so blessed and certain. To put it another way, the believer's hope is not what might be true. It is indeed what every child of God already has. Hope for all eternity is the hope.

A very good friend of mine, who has since gone to heaven, called it "going home." Heaven and eternity with God and His people is the believer's certainty.[7] How wonderful this truth is!

The Bible Speaks of Three Heavens

In some books on occult philosophy, angelic rulers are assigned to seven heavens: the first heaven—Gabriel; the second heaven—Zachariel and Raphael; the third heaven—Anahel; the fourth heaven—Michael; the fifth heaven—Sandalphon; the sixth heaven—Zachiel; and the seventh heaven—Cassiel.[8]

The Bible, on the other hand, teaches that there are only three heavens. About 14 years before Paul wrote 2 Corinthians, he had a vision about which he wrote:

> I knew a man in Christ above fourteen years ago, (whether in the body, I cannot tell; or whether out of the body, I cannot tell: God knoweth;) such an one caught up to the third heaven (2 Cor. 12:2).

What are these three heavens and in which of them do angels dwell?

---

7   Mal and Lacy Couch, *Going Home* (Springfield, MO: 21st Century Press, 2006).
8   Gustav Davidson, *A Dictionary of Angels* (New York: Free, 1967), p. 340.

We know for a number of reasons from Scripture that holy angels do make their home in heaven. They are described as *the heavenly hosts* in Luke 2:13. Jesus spoke of "the angels which are in heaven" (Mark 13:32). An angel "descended from heaven . . . and rolled back the stone" in front of Jesus' grave (Matt. 28:2). The Apostle Paul wrote that "though we, or an angel from heaven" came and preached a foreign gospel, it should not be believed (Gal. 1:8).

We know, too, that when the eternal Son of God became man, He "was made a little lower than the angels" (Heb. 2:9). This means He passed through the realm of angels in order to take on a human nature so He could die for humankind. And when Jesus returned to God the Father, He "passed into the heavens" (Heb. 4:14). This would imply that angels dwell in the second heaven, though they have access to the third for special ministries (cf. Isa. 6:3, Rev. 5:11; 7:11). The first heaven, then, is the atmospheric heaven; the second is the stellar heaven and home of angels; and the third is the abode of God.

Evangelicals are divided on whether holy angels have their home in the second heaven or the third. Some holy angels, it seems, do reside in God's presence. Examples might be those Isaiah saw in his vision (cf. Isa. 6:1-6) and Gabriel, who stands in the presence of God (Luke 1:19).

Angels do not dwell where God dwells, though they may indeed have access to Him. We need to remember, too, that Satan desired to ascend to where God dwells (Isa. 14:13).

It is very important for our study of heaven and hell that we take the time to think further about the nature and importance of angels, since they play such a large role in the future with regard to both of these eternal destinations.

Humans and angels have a number of similarities. Both are created by God. Both were created in a state of creaturely perfection. All that God made He pronounced very good. As we have seen, angels have personality.

People possess personality as well. Angels and humankind sinned during their appointed times of probation. The angels sinned individually by following Satan in his great sin of pride and rebellion against God (cf. Isa. 14:13-14). The human race sinned in and through Adam (cf. Gen. 3: Rom. 5:12). Also, both are "servants of the most high God" (Dan. 3:26).

Neither angels nor humans are to be worshiped. Both are to worship God alone. John the apostle was so impressed and overwhelmed by what an angel showed him of the New Jerusalem that he fell down to worship the angel. Quickly the angel said to him, "See *thou do it* not: for I am thy fellowservant, and of thy brethren the prophets, and of them which keep the sayings of this book: worship God" (Rev 22:9). In his letter to the Colossian Christians, Paul made it crystal clear that angels are never to be worshiped (Col. 2:18).

However, humans and angelic beings also have many dissimilarities. No Divine grace was extended to angels who sinned by following Satan and his rebellion. Those who thus sinned were confirmed in their wickedness, and those who refused to follow Satan were confirmed in their holiness.

Angels are of a higher order of creation than people. In His incarnation, Christ the Redeemer passed through the angelic order; He "was made a little lower than the angels . . . that he by the grace of God should taste death for every man" (Heb. 2:9). To provide salvation for the world, Christ needed to become temporarily lower than angels. Thus, the human race is of a lower order of creation than angels. In the future eternal state, Christians will "shall judge angels" (1 Cor. 6:3—thus indicating that believers will occupy a higher position than angels.

Angels do not propagate and are therefore distinct from people in this regard. They do not need to reproduce since they do not die as humans do. As indicated earlier, no salvation has been extended to angels. Holy angels observe salvation but do not fully comprehend it (1 Pet. 1:12). And we cannot understand it either. All we can say is that it took a miracle to save our souls. But we can and should rejoice in it and share the gospel with our lives and our lips. It is "the power of God unto salvation to every one that believeth" (Rom. 1:16).

Though people and angels are both creatures of God, there is nevertheless a great difference between them in relation to God. Angels are never said to be made in the image of God and after God's likeness, yet man is. Some believe angels were created in God's image,[9] though this is not specifically stated in Scripture. This idea is usually based on the fact that both have personalities, and personality is what is meant by *the image of God*.

Now, if that is all that is involved in the image of God, the conclusion would be a reasonable one. However, the meaning of the image of God in man involves much more, including man's responsibility to rule over the earth (Gen. 1:26). The image is also related to *righteousness* and *holiness* (Eph. 4:24) and *knowledge* (Col. 3: 10; cf. Rom. 8:29), as well as immortality.[10]

Holy Angelic Activities in Heaven

Seventeen Old Testament books make 108 references to angels, and 17 New Testament books refer to angels 175 times. Strangely, many questions about these spirit beings are not answered in the Bible. However, we do have enough information to establish a Biblical doctrine of angels and to evaluate the current craze, the angel mania, that is upon us.

The English word *angel* comes from the Hebrew word *malak* and the Greek *angelos*. Both of these words mean *messenger*. The terms are used for spirit beings without physical bodies and for human messengers. The context tells us which is in view.

In this section, we are only concerned with the messengers who

---

9 C. Fred Dickason, *Angels Elect and Evil* (Chicago: Moody, 1975), p. 32.
10 James Oliver Buswell, *A Systematic Theology of the Christian Religion* (Grand Rapids: Zondervan, 1971), pp. 231-42.

are spirit beings; furthermore, holy angels are our concern, not Satan and demons. The latter two will be discussed later.

Except for the first in the list of angelic activities which follows, there is no significance in the order in which these activities are presented. God's ministering spirits are discussed first because their work of ministering is their primary role. As ministering spirits, these messengers carry out God's bidding.

Limited examples of the activities named will be cited. There is some overlap in these activities. More activities could be added; but only the major ones are included.

Ministering spirits of God. The Hebrew and Greek words translated as *angel* reveal their chief assignment. The writer of Hebrews affirms that the holy angels are "ministering spirits, sent forth to minister for them who shall be heirs of salvation" (Heb. 1:14). They are God's "ministers" (1:7).

We certainly do not know all the specific ways in which holy angels minister to believers, but we are assured in Scripture that they do minister to God's children. Many of the following activities serve as illustrations of some of the ways they minister.

The ministries to and for Christ by angels is another great area of ministry not to be overlooked. Again, the book of Hebrews stresses these activities, thereby highlighting that Christ is "so much better than the angels" (Heb. 1:4).

They give messages from God. Abraham's nephew, Lot, lived among the wicked Sodomites (Gen. 19). God sent two angels to deliver Lot from destruction. They told Lot to take his wife and daughters and get out of the city before God's judgment fell on it.

The men of Sodom intended to sexually molest Lot's two guests. Neither the Sodomites nor Lot realized at first that the two messengers were angels of God appearing as men. These angels, faithful in their service to God, surrounded Lot until he was safe outside the wicked city. These same two angels not only carried God's message to Lot but also were used of God to bring judgment on the wicked Sodomites.

A second example of angels acting as God's messengers was when the God-fearing Cornelius, a centurion of an Italian regiment, "saw in a vision ... an angel of God" (Acts 10:3). The angel spoke to Cornelius directly and specifically. A special message was on its way.

The angel told Cornelius to dispatch some men to Joppa to seek out Simon Peter. The angel even gave specific instruction on where Peter could be found. When the angel concluded his message, he left. Cornelius wasted no time doing precisely as the angel told him. He explained the assignment to three men (two servants and a soldier, v. 7) and "sent them to Joppa" (v. 8).

Before these men arrived at Peter's house, God gave Peter a vision. A sheet came down to earth on which were all kinds of four-footed animals, crawling creatures, and birds. A voice told Peter to kill and eat them. He refused to do so because the animals on the sheet were unclean according to the Jewish Law. The voice said that Peter should not call unclean what God had cleansed, and then the sheet was lifted up toward heaven.

About that time, after God had prepared Peter, the three men arrived. They rehearsed what the angel had told Cornelius and said that Peter was invited to come to Cornelius' house and give him God's message. Although Peter was a Jew and Jews did not associate in that way with Gentiles, he went and told Cornelius and his relatives and friends all about Christ's death and resurrection, and the commission Christ gave to the apostles. As Peter spoke, the Holy Spirit fell on the Gentiles as He had in Jerusalem on the day of Pentecost (v. 44). All of this took place because an angel gave God's message to Cornelius.

They give guidance and instruction. At the bidding of his father Isaac, Jacob left Beersheba and headed for Haran to find a wife. One night, as he slept with a stone for a pillow, he had a dream in which he saw a ladder reaching from earth to heaven. He saw "the angels of God ascending and descending on it" (Gen. 28:12). In Jacob's dream, God stood beside him. The Lord assured Jacob that he was the God-appointed heir of the covenant given to Abraham and Isaac.

Jacob was convinced that God was at work in him and would use him mightily. The very place where he slept, saw the ladder and the angels and heard God's message was sacred to him. Jacob saw the place as the very gateway to heaven through which angels passed to do their earthly chores. He changed the name of that place from Luz to Bethel (28:19), which means "the house of God."

Later, God told Jacob to go back from Haran to his homeland (31:11, 13). When he was on his way home, "the angels of God met him" again and assured him of God's presence with him (32:1-2).

God told Moses He would send an angel to guide the Israelites through the wilderness (Exod. 23:20; 32:34) to the land of Canaan (23:23; 33:2). Here, a single angel led the entire nation of Israel for 40 years.

The New Testament includes similar examples of holy angels giving guidance and instruction from God to man. For example, Philip was led to the Ethiopian eunuch by instruction from "an angel of the Lord" (Acts 8:26). The angel gave him specific directions with vivid descriptions of conditions around the place. This angel must have known when the man from Ethiopia would be passing by there. He knew too what he would be doing—reading from the prophecy of Isaiah. God sent His angel to bring Philip and the court official from Ethiopia together so that the Ethiopian might hear the gospel and become a child of God.

They deliver from danger. As the infant church, which began on the day of Pentecost, grew and expanded, the unbelieving Jewish authorities opposed the apostles and the early Christians. Out of jealousy, the high priest and the Sadducees "laid their hands on the apostles, and put them in the common prison" (Acts 5:17-18).

During the night as the apostles slept, an angel not only opened the gates of the jail and took the apostles out but also told them what they were to do. They were to give the temple authorities the same message they preached before they were incarcerated.

But when the apostles did this, they were again brought before the unbelieving Jewish leaders and warned not to speak anymore in the name of Jesus. The apostles listened politely and then proceeded to do exactly what they were told not to do (vv. 21-42).

On another occasion, Peter was put in prison by Herod Agrippa's order. The wicked king had already put James, John's brother, to death. He saw that this pleased the Jewish leaders, so he arrested Peter also and assigned four squads of four soldiers each to guard him. Herod planned to bring Peter before the people after the Passover and then no doubt have him put to death.

A band of believers heard about this and began a concerted prayer effort. Peter, bound with chains, was sleeping soundly between two of the guards. Suddenly, an angel of the Lord appeared to him. A bright light shone in the dark, dingy place. Arousing Peter from sleep, the angel told him to get up quickly. Peter thought he was seeing a vision. He obeyed the angel, and when he did, the chains that bound him fell off (vv. 1-7).

Then, the angel told Peter to put his cloak around him, put on his sandals, and follow him. Peter did so, still thinking he was having a vision. He followed the angel past two guards and watched the huge iron gates open miraculously.

Once outside, the angel disappeared just as suddenly as he had appeared. When Peter realized what had happened, he went to Mary's house, who was John's mother, and discovered that a prayer meeting for him was in session. Those praying could not believe that their prayers had been answered (12:8-17).

When Herod discovered all this, he had the guards led off to execution. God later sent another angel, or perhaps the same one, to strike Herod, causing Herod to die because he would not acknowledge the God of heaven. So the one who had God's servants killed was himself killed by one of the Lord's angelic servants (12:18-23).

They view human affairs. The Bible records several examples of angels observing the lives and activities of God's people. Paul the apostle was setting forth himself as an example of doing Christ-honoring Christian service. He wrote,

> For I think that God hath set forth us the apostles last, as it were appointed to death: for we are made a spectacle unto the world, and to angels, and to men (1 Cor. 4:9).

This observation by angels indicates their interest in the work of redemption, even though they are not recipients of it.

A similar reminder was given to the women in the Corinthian church. They, too, were being watched by angels. Because of this, they were to cover their heads at worship (1 Cor. 11:10). Why holy angels were concerned about women's head coverings is not clear.

Paul wrote to the believers in Ephesus that his ministry would cause angelic beings to see the wisdom of God in His ways with people. His statement about "the principalities and powers in the heavenly places" (Eph. 3:10) refers to angels. In rabbinic thought, these terms, as well as "might, and dominion" (1:21), described the order and rank among angels.

The Apostle Paul also solemnly charged Timothy, his son in the faith, about local church affairs, and Paul made this charge not only "before God, and the Lord Jesus Christ," but also before "the elect angels" (1 Tim. 5:21). This, too, indicates angelic observance of human affairs.

Peter wrote that human salvation is something into which the angels desire to look into (1 Pet. 1:12). The Greek verb used here (*parakupto)* means *to stoop or bend down* (or *stretch forward the head)*—to look so as to get a better view of something. The same word is used to describe the apostles' search for the body of Jesus at the tomb of Joseph of Arimathea (Luke 24:12; John 20:5).

Finally, God's angels rejoice when sinners accept the Savior as their substitute for sin (Luke 15:10).

They protect God's people. In the Bible, angels did more than deliver messages and observe human affairs. They were also personally involved in protecting God's people in times of great need.

Two familiar incidents that are recorded in the Old Testament illustrate this work of God's angels.

The first of these is the fiery-furnace incident of Shadrach, Meshach and Abednego in the book of Daniel. We cannot help but wonder what they thought would happen to them when they refused to follow the king's orders. They made it clear that whether God would deliver them from the furnace or let them die by the flames, they would not serve Nebuchadnezzar's gods (Dan. 3:16-18). The king soon discovered not only that the three did not burn in his furnace but that a fourth person was also with them. He said the fourth had a "form . . . like the Son of God" (Dan. 3:25). This was God's special agent, a holy angel, sent to protect His servants.

Some years later, Daniel refused to worship pagan gods, just as his three friends had done. Darius, the king, was caught in a trap, and in order to save face, he allowed his friend Daniel to be thrown to the lions. The king could not wait until morning to see what had happened to Daniel. Had Daniel's God protected him or not? God had saved Daniel, and He did this by sending His angel and shutting the lions' mouths (Dan. 6:22)

As already noted, centuries earlier, an angel guarded (and guided) Israel in the wilderness wanderings (Ex. 23:20).

We have observed how holy angels delivered the apostles and Peter from prison on two separate occasions in the New Testament (Acts 5:17-24; 12:3-12). Those angelic deliverances also illustrate God's protection of His own.

Another New Testament story gives account of an angel helping the Apostle Paul. As Paul was being taken to Rome as a prisoner, the ship he was on encountered a severe storm and the lives of everyone on board were in danger. Paul stood boldly before them all and gave this message: "And now I exhort you to be of good cheer: for there shall be no loss of any man's life among you . . . for there stood by me this night the angel of God, whose I am, and whom I serve, Saying, Fear not, Paul; thou must be brought before Caesar; and, lo, God hath given thee all them that sail with thee" (Acts 27:22-24). Here, an angel encouraged Paul and kept everyone on the ship alive during the terrifying storm.

They provide strength and encouragement. Elijah was running from Jezebel, the wicked wife of Ahab. After about one day's journey into the desert, the prophet came to a juniper tree and begged God to let him die (1 Kings 19:3-4). As he prayed, Elijah fell asleep. He was awakened by an angel touching him and telling him to get up and eat.

When Elijah got up as the angel had instructed, he saw a cake of bread and a container of water. He ate and then lay down again. A second time, the strange creature came and touched Elijah and told him to get up and eat. The angel had prepared a meal for the prophet and provided water for him to drink. Elijah's physical strength was restored for 40 days and 40 nights (19:5-8).

The angel Gabriel told the fearful Zacharias that his wife, Elisabeth, would have a son whose name was to be John (Luke 1:8-9, 11-13). Zacharias was from the priestly tribe of Levi and Elisabeth was a descendant of Aaron. Presumably, they were each about 60 years old at the time. The angel ministered to Zacharias by calming his fears regarding what he had seen and heard.

The same angel ministered to the virgin Mary in a similar way (Luke 1:27-28, 30-31). Mary, too, was fearful, and she wondered, "How could I, a virgin, ever be pregnant?" The heavenly messenger said to her,

Fear not, Mary: for thou hast found favor with God. And, behold, thou shalt conceive in thy womb, and bring forth a son, and shalt call his name JESUS. (Luke 1:30-31)

Like Elijah and Zacharias, she was also encouraged by an angel.

They execute judgment. In reviewing the history of the Israelites, the psalmist Asaph gave this description of the plagues that God inflicted on the Egyptians:

He cast upon them the fierceness of his anger, wrath, and indignation, and trouble, by sending evil angels *among* them (Ps. 78:49).

The angel who led and protected the Israelites in the wilderness was also involved in helping them destroy the inhabitants of Canaan (Ex. 33:2).

Jesus also discussed a time when the angels will execute judgement. When talking to his disciples, He told and then explained the parable of the wheat and the tares (Matt. 13:24-30, 37-43). The gathering and burning of the tares, He said, would involve Him and His angels.

He explained,

The Son of man shall send forth his angels, and they shall gather out of his kingdom all things that offend, and them which do iniquity; And shall cast them into a furnace of fire: there shall be wailing and gnashing of teeth (Matt. 13:41-42).

On another occasion, Jesus made a similar announcement. He said the Son of Man would come to the earth "in the glory of His Father with His angels; and then he shall reward every man according to his works" (Matt. 16:27). In other words, the angels of God will assist Him in His work of judgment in the future.

The book of Revelation records a number of examples of angels executing Divine judgment. John the apostle saw four angels in control of the elements of nature on the earth (Rev. 7:1). In his vision of Armageddon, he also saw an angel with power over fire (14:18). Seven angels each blew a trumpet to announce a series of judgments (Rev. 8-9). An eighth angel came in John's vision and held a golden censer. John writes that "there was given unto him much incense, that he should offer it with the prayers of all saints upon the golden altar which was before the throne" (8:3). When each angel blew his trumpet, awful Divine punishment came upon the world by the wrath of God.

Another outstanding example of angelic involvement in the outpouring of future judgment is found in Revelation 15–16. Again, John saw seven angels who held seven vials of Divine wrath to be poured out upon the world. In turn, each angel emptied his vial of God's wrath onto people and nations.

Many other angels are mentioned by John in Revelation. God will employ them to carry out the world's rendezvous with Divine judgment in the future tribulation.

They praise God. One of the chief activities of holy angels is giving worship to God. The Bible repeatedly speaks of angels praising the Lord. The psalmist called on his own heart to praise God (Ps. 103:1). Then, he begged the angels to bless Him. In doing so, he described these angels as ones who "excel in strength," those who "do His commandments" and who are constantly following "the voice of His word" (103:20).

In Isaiah's vision, the seraphim were occupied constantly with worshiping God (Isa. 6:1-7). One of the seraphim cried out to another, saying, "Holy, holy, holy, *is* the LORD of hosts" (6:3). The seraphim each had six wings—two covered their faces, two their feet, and two were used to fly. One of the angels in Isaiah's vision flew to the prophet and took a burning coal from the altar in the vision, touched Isaiah's mouth and told him he was cleansed and his sin forgiven (6:6-7). The angel did not forgive him. God alone forgave him, and the angel simply announced the forgiveness to Isaiah.

Christ's superiority to angels is stressed by the writer of Hebrews in the beginning of that book. God the Father never said to an angel, "Thou art my Son" (Heb. 1:5), but the Lord Jesus Christ is the eternal Son of God. Angels were given the assignment of worshiping Christ the Son of God when He came into the world. The decree was to "let all the angels of God worship Him" (1:6). They did then and continue to do so today.

John described the angels he saw in his vision as "four beasts" (Rev. 4:8). These angels are probably the same creatures that are seen in Ezekiel's vision in Ezekiel 1:1-28 and the cherubim in Ezekiel 10:1-22. They never cease to say essentially what the seraphim said in Isaiah's vision: "Holy, holy, holy, LORD God Almighty, which was, and is, and is to come" (Rev. 4:8).

In Revelation 5:12, an innumerable company of angels were heard saying, "Worthy is the Lamb." This song of praise resulted from the fact that Christ, the Lamb of God, was worthy to open the sealed book, which no one else was worthy to open.

The angels of God serve as examples for us as God's children to never cease in worshiping God the Father, God the Son and God the Holy Spirit. Instead of always asking God to bless us in all our needs, we need to bless Him and praise Him even when we are hurting and things are not going our way. There is no more important activity in which we can be involved than the worship of our great God.

Never does Scripture give any sanction to humans praying to angels or worshiping them. On the contrary, there are injunctions against such behavior. Those who did worship angels in the early days of the church were rebuked sharply by Paul (Col. 2:18). On a separate occasion, the Apostle John himself fell down and began to worship an angel. But that angel promptly rebuked him. The angel said,

> See *thou do it* not: for I am thy fellowservant, and of thy brethren the prophets, and of them which keep the sayings of this book: worship God. (Rev. 22:9; also see 19:10)

They guard believers. The ministry of holy angels on behalf of God's people is clearly taught and presented in Scripture. The ministries we have surveyed lend support to the reality of guardian angels. They, in fact, do protect God's people in times of great need.

Some secular theorists go far beyond Scripture and assign guardian angels to the planets in our solar system. Seven of these angels are named, along with the planet over which each one is said to preside. Rahatiel is said to be the chief angel of the planets. Raphael is over the sun, Gabriel is over the moon, and five of the planets each has a named angel: Michael is over Mercury, Aniel over Venus, Samel over Mars, Zadkiel over Jupiter, and Kafziel over Saturn.[11] These ideas, however, are not taught in the Bible.

Notice that the term *guardian angel* does not appear in Scripture. That, of course, does not mean that such beings do not exist. Though the term is sometimes used to speak of angelic ministry to adults, it is usually used with reference to infants and young children. The familiar Christian artist's visualization of one or more angels rescuing a child from great danger portrays this concept.

Some believe that each child has one holy angel assigned to him or her by God. Others believe each child has more than one angel. Still, others believe that holy angels have the care of infants and children as their general assignment rather than one or more angels being responsible for a specific child.

As discussed earlier in this book, the key verse in support of guardian angels for infants and children is Matthew 18:10. When speaking to His disciples, Jesus illustrated the need for childlike faith as He called a child to His side. He then said to them,

> Take heed that ye despise not one of these little ones; for I say unto you, That in heaven their angels do always behold the face of my Father which is in heaven. (Matt. 18:10)

---

11 Davidson, *A Dictionary of Angels*, p. 343.

Rather than one or more angels attending each child, this verse may mean that angels carry out a general ministry to children by representing them before God, as they appear in God's presence (beholding His *face*) in heaven.[12]

Do angels minister to adult believers also? Indeed, they do! The writer of Hebrews affirmed this clearly when he wrote that "ministering spirits, [are] sent forth to minister for them who shall be heirs of salvation" (Heb. 1:14). The question is not, "Do angels do this?" but rather, "When does this ministry begin?" We are not told specifically, but it seems natural that it would begin as soon as life begins.

Further support for the ministry of guardian angels over God's people is in both the Old and New Testaments. Here are some specific verses bearing on the subject. We have referred to some of these earlier.

When the prophet Elijah was fleeing from Jezebel for his life, he lay down to sleep under a juniper tree in the desert. There, an angel came and ministered to him (1 Kings 19:5).

The psalmist said the Lord would give a host of His angels charge over His people to guard them in all their ways (Ps. 91:11) and protect them from harm (Ps. 12:6-7).

After surviving a night in a den of lions, Daniel tells King Darius, "My God hath sent his angel, and hath shut the lions' mouths, that they have not hurt me" (Dan. 6:22).

After the wise men who worshiped baby Jesus left to return home, "the angel of the Lord appeareth to Joseph in a dream" (Matt. 2:13). The angel told him to take Mary and baby Jesus and escape to Egypt. After Herod died, an angel of the Lord appeared again to Joseph telling him to return to his homeland (2:19-20).

---

12 See Roy B. Zuck, *Precious in His Sight: Childhood and Children in the Bible* (Grand Rapids: Baker, 1996), pp. 210-11. Others say "their angels" in Matthew 18:10 refers to the spirits of little children who died. However, the Bible gives no support to the common idea that people become angels when they die.

As Herbert Lockyer points out, knowing that angels guard us can ease our concerns in life. He writes,

> It is to be feared that the presence and power of Angels are not as real to us as they should be. While we have no way of knowing how often our feet are directed into right paths, or how often we are guarded from harm, seen or unseen, or how subject we are to angelic suggestion, our invisible companions are ever at hand. They form our protective shield, and over and above them is the everlasting God and Father they serve and we love. So why should we charge our souls with care?[13]

As we think of guardian angels watching over us, we need to be sure we keep our eyes on the God who sent them, not on the angels themselves.

Summary. The Bible clearly presents angels as God's worshipers and messengers—those who carry out His bidding, assisting Him and His people. They themselves never sinned and, therefore, have never experienced God's saving grace, but their ministries toward humans who did sin and have been redeemed are abundant.

Two of the angels' many activities are their ministry for God and their praise of God. Besides these two chief functions in relation to God, we saw that they have many responsibilities in relation to people: delivering messages from God to individuals, guiding and instructing God's people, delivering them from danger and death, observing human affairs, protecting God's people, providing strength and encouragement for God's special servants and executing Divine judgment on the deserving.

Some say there are certain angels for each day of the week and even each hour of the day and night. Some even believe angels are assigned to animals. Over tame beasts there is the angel Behemiel, while Thegri is the angel assigned to wild beasts. Birds, too, are under angelic supervision, we are told. Arael is the angel over birds. The dove, however, is the only creature who has its own angel, namely, Alphun. There is no Biblical support for these ideas.

---

13 Herbert Lockyer, *All the Angels in the Bible* (Peabody, MA: Hendrickson, 1996), p. 68.

There are many other legends and traditions regarding angels, which should cause us to exercise a great deal of discernment when we hear them. A woman reported that she was visited by four angels one night as she contemplated all the things she still needed to do before she died. She said she knew the angels were there in the room with her because her golden retriever saw them. And she said she knew that because the dog nosed one of the angels out of his way so he could go to sleep on his favorite spot in the room.[14]

Some think that angels take care of plants and trees, and that this holds the key as to how they are formed. A so-called nature spirit supposedly builds plants and trees from the plans formulated by angels.

Angels are currently watching over countries, states, and even cities, according to many people. These are called Archons or *rulers*. These spirit beings reportedly help guide the primary mission of that place so as to make it more successful in realizing its goal.

The weather and seasons of the year are controlled by angels, some insist.

Present-day angel theorists insist angels have their own celestial alphabets that are variations of the Hebrew alphabet. One stated: "Who knows what masterpieces some may have written for the pleasure of the angelic realm?"[15]

People frequently report having received some communication from angels. This takes varied forms. It may be simply an extremely strong feeling, the communication of certain facts or a physical intervention by an angel's hand or body. Usually this latter form comes to keep the person from danger or even death. Some report they have heard angel voices giving instruction. They urge all who hear these voices to obey them.

What we believe about angels must be based on the Word of God. None of our doctrines should be built on an experience someone claims to

14   Sophy Burnham, *A Book of Angels* (New York: Ballantine, 1990), pp. 133-36.
15   Carolyn Trickey-Bapty *The Book of Angels* (Ambler, PA: Ottenheimer, 1994), p. 45

have had. Simply because someone says he or she saw or heard an angel does not mean what they saw or heard was, in fact, an angel. It is not unusual, for example, to have a dream in which "people" are seen and voices "heard." I have had such dreams myself. When we awake, we discover that what we saw was real only in our dreams.

Angels continue to be God's ministering spirit. There can be no doubt about that. But do they minister in the same way they did when the Bible was in the making?

We do not know which specific ministries of angels continue today and which do not. We can be sure that some do not occur today, but does that mean none of them do? Hardly. But since the canon of Scripture is closed, angels are no longer being used of God to give His revelation to people. If angels were still giving inspired messages, this would mean the Scriptures are not complete.

Are angels still opening prison doors as they did for the apostles? Do those who are innocent but judged guilty escape the electric chair or lethal injection by the intervention of an angel? We do not put criminals in fiery furnaces or dens of lions today, but do these same kinds of deliverances occur today?

While we can be sure that some activities of angels no longer occur, others may be falsely imagined as taking place. It is also strikingly strange that those reporting and recording angelic sightings and voices rarely, if ever, see or hear them meting out judgment on offenders. Instead, they are seen with happy, helpful messages, always offering assistance to individuals. Yet, in the Bible, angels often carried out God's judgments and will do so in the future. Why not now?

If we would each keep our focus on Jesus, we would be fulfilling the Biblical mandate. He is the living Word of God. Must we know if an angel (or angels) is involved in particular areas of our lives? We know God has promised to care for us. Is that not enough? What difference does it make whether we "see" or "hear" an angel?

Focusing on angels and what they can or cannot do keeps us from being occupied with Jesus. Though the Bible has much to say about angels, at no time were people intended to be caught up with angel mania. We are to focus on the Lord, not angels. Angels have never witnessed for Christ. That is our task. Angels have never prayed for lost souls. That is our job. Angels do not distribute the Word of God to people either. That is a privilege God has given us.

The songwriter put it all in perspective in this song:

Holy, Holy, Is What the Angels Sing

There is singing up in heaven such as we have never known,
Where the angels sing the praises of the Lamb upon the throne;
Their sweet harps are ever tuneful and their voices always clear,
Oh, that we might be more like them while we serve the Master here.

Refrain
Holy, holy, is what the angels sing,
And I expect to help them make the courts of heaven ring;
But when I sing redemption's story, they will fold their wings,
For angels never felt the joys that our salvation brings.

Then the angels stand and listen, for they cannot join that song,
Like the sound of many waters, by that happy, bloodwashed throng;
For they sing about great trials, battles fought and vict'ries won,
And they praise their get Redeemer, who hath said to them, "Well done."

So, although I'm not an angel, yet I know that over there
I will join a blessed chorus that the angels cannot share;
I will sing about my Saviour, who upon dark Calvary
Freely pardoned my transgressions, died to set a sinner free.[16]

---

16 Johnson Oatman, Jr. and John R. Sweney, *Sing Men, Number Two* (Wheaton, IL: Singspiration, 1950), p. 57. Used by permission.

SOME BIBLICAL DESCRIPTIONS OF HEAVEN

After His resurrection, Jesus appeared to His disciples who were perplexed and confused about the reality of Jesus' empty tomb (Luke 24:1-44). He reminded them of what the Scriptures predicted about His resurrection. They must have forgotten what He had taught them. Then, Jesus led them to Bethany and blessed them. While He was doing this, "he was parted from them, and carried up into heaven" (Luke 24:50-51).

Four specific passages of Scripture describe heaven, where Jesus currently resides and where all who are born again will spend eternity with Him.

2 Corinthians 5:1-4

For we know that if our earthly house of this tabernacle were dissolved, we have a building of God, an house not made with hands, eternal in the heavens.

Obviously, this passage refers to believers who will spend eternity with God and all the occupants of heaven. How thankful we should be that even though we still face death here on earth, we will not face death in heaven.

2 Corinthians 12:2-4

I knew a man in Christ above fourteen years ago, (whether in the body, I cannot tell; or whether out of the body, I cannot tell: God knoweth;) such an one caught up to the third heaven. And I knew such a man, (whether in the body, or out of the body, I cannot tell: God knoweth;) How that he was caught up into paradise, and heard unspeakable words, which it is not lawful for a man to utter.

Imagine, in heaven, those who have accepted Christ as Savior will experience untold blessing for all eternity. That truth should embolden us and encourage us every step of the way.

Philippians 1:23-24

For I am in a strait betwixt two, having a desire to depart, and to be with Christ; which is far better: Nevertheless to abide in the flesh is more needful for you.

Heaven is far better than anything here on earth because there we will be with our Savior forever.

Hebrews 11:13-16

These all died in faith, not having received the promises, but having seen them afar off, and were persuaded of *them*, and embraced *them*, and confessed that they were strangers and pilgrims on the earth. For they that say such things declare plainly that they seek a country. And truly, if they had been mindful of that *country* from whence they came out, they might have had opportunity to have returned. But now they desire a better *country*, that is, an heavenly: wherefore God is not ashamed to be called their God: for he hath prepared for them a city.

The child of God's faith will be turned into sight. Heaven is indeed far better than anything here on earth. All believers will spend eternity with God!

THE BELIEVER'S BLESSED HOPE

Robert Gromacki gives this helpful truth concerning the believer's blessed hope:

One of the most beautiful words in all of the English language is "hope." The young woman hoards silverware and china, in her "hope chest," looking forward to engagement and marriage. A family hangs on to the words of hope from the doctor's mouth as a loved one goes into surgery. Children hope for those special Christmas gifts.[17]

Hope is also one of the basic Christian words comparable to faith and love (1 Cor. 13:13). Paul said, "For we are saved by hope: but hope that is seen is not hope: for what a man seeth, why doth he yet hope for?" (Rom. 8:24).

The Apostle Paul's word to the local church in Thessalonica tells us how believers will *be caught up together with* Christ when He comes to take the body of Christ, the church, to be with Him forever.

Paul writes,

> For the Lord Himself shall descend from heaven with a shout, with the voice of the archangel, and with the trump of God: and the dead in Christ shall rise first: Then we which are alive and remain shall be caught up together with them in the clouds, to meet the Lord in the air: and so shall we ever be with the Lord. Wherefore comfort one another with these words (1 Thess. 4:16-18).

What we learn from these words from Paul while he was on his second missionary journey should encourage us to keep on keeping on. Oh, what a blessed hope that is for every child of God.

How wonderful it is that in the future there will be a new heaven and a new earth that will endure forever. On the other hand, how sobering it is that the unsaved will be in everlasting torment and fire that will never be extinguished.

Robert Peterson has helped us to understand what is meant by "their worm shall not die" and "neither shall their fire be quenched" in Isaiah 66:24:

> To show contempt, a victorious army would leave the bodies of its foes unburied on the battlefield. To be subject to such exposure was considered a disgrace. It denied the deceased a proper burial. Worst, the

17 Robert G. Gromacki, *Are These the Last Days?* (Old Tappan, NJ: Fleming H. Revell Co., 1970), p. 51.

birds would feast on the remains. Worst of all, what the birds began the worms would finish.[18]

CONCLUSION

All of us have made appointments. We do this many times. We have appointments with doctors, dentists, lawyers, business associates and friends. Oh, I almost forgot, how about the date of April 15 every year? We sometimes fail to keep our appointments and even forget we have one sometimes; I suspect it all depends on how important we think the appointment really is.

Whether we want to admit it or not, all of us do have an appointment given to us by God. The Bible puts it this way, "And as it is appointed unto men once to die, but after this the judgment" (Heb. 9:27).

I really hope and pray you never forget that you do have this appointment with God Almighty; all of us do. There is absolutely no exception. Whether we are young, middle-aged or older, and whether we like it or not, we all have this Divine appointment with our Creator.

This same loving and righteous God has told us in His Word how we all need to prepare to meet Him. God the Father has sent His Son, the Lord Jesus Christ, to pay the penalty for the sin of all mankind.

The Apostle John put it this way,

> "For God so loved the world, that he gave His only begotten Son, that whosoever believeth in Him should not perish, but have everlasting life. For God sent not His Son into the world to condemn the world; but that the world through Him might be saved" (John 3:16-17).

---

18 Robert A. Peterson, *Hell on Trial: The Case for Eternal Punishment* (Phillipsburg, NJ: P&R Publishing, 1995), pp. 31-32.

PART 2

HELL

INTRODUCTION

Both the Old and New Testaments describe hell using many different terms such as: sheol, hades, tartaros, gehenna, retribution, prison, chains, stripes, weeping and gnashing of teeth, abyss or bottomless pit, outer darkness, destruction, torments, worm, fire, second death, wrath of God and eternity.[19]

The final state of the wicked is described under the figures of *everlasting fire* (Matt. 25:41), the *pit* or *bottomless pit* (Rev. 9:2, 11); *outer darkness* (Matt. 25:30); the *wrath* of God (Rom. 2:5); *the second death* (Rev. 21:8); *everlasting destruction from the presence of the Lord* (2 Thess. 1:9); and *eternal damnation* (Mark 3:29).

Is there really an actual hell created by God? How can that be, you might ask, since, according to the Bible, God is love and He is gracious?

---

19 For further discussion of these terms I recommend Tim Lahaye and Ed Hindson, eds., *The Popular Encyclopedia of Bible Prophecy* (Eugene, OR: Harvest House Publishers, 2004), pp. 134-38.

Scripture does speak clearly about God and His love for all mankind, but it also speaks clearly about heaven and hell. So, the answer to the question is an emphatic *yes*—there is an eternal hell for the unsaved.

We might also ask why God created this world, as well as who is going to heaven forever and who is going to hell forever. Not all who claim to know the true God agree on the answers to these questions, as we shall see.

SOME VIEWS OF HELL AMONG BIBLE BELIEVERS

Many scholars and lay people have held, and still hold, to the belief that there is a heaven to be gained and a hell to be shunned.

The publisher of a book entitled *Four Views of Hell* said this about the book in its Foreword:

> Probably the most disturbing concept in Christian tradition is the prospect that one day vast numbers of people will be consigned to hell. Almost everyone has friends or family members—people we dearly love—who are outside the faith and who, if they die in this condition, will be cast away from the presence of God. So disturbing is the idea of hell that most pastors and church members simply ignore the doctrine of final retribution, preferring to talk in vague terms about a separation of the wicked from the righteous.

> But what is hell? A literal place of flame and smoke? A banishment from God? Annihilation? Is there such a place as purgatory where people are readied for the presence of God? . . . Those who have always wondered about the nature of hell will find the differing perspectives interesting and informative.[20]

First, Dr. John F. Walvoord, past president of Dallas Theological Seminary,

---

20 John Walvoord, William Crockett, Zachary Hayes, Clark Pinnock; Ed.by William Crockett, *Four Views on Hell* (Grand Rapids: Zondervan, 1992), p. 7.

presented the literal view of hell in this book. He began by discussing the problems with the concept of eternal punishment for those outside of Christ and the various views held on the subject of hell. The view he holds is that hell is real and "punitive not redemptive." He deals extensively with the Old Testament teaching on hell as well as the New Testament teaching.

Walvoord writes:

> To some, that the idea of "forever" does not always mean an infinite duration in time may seem to be an unnecessary concession to the opponents of eternal punishment. But like the word "all," this word has to be interpreted in its context; and where the context itself limits the duration, this needs to be recognized in fairness to the text. At the same time, however, an important principle must be observed all throughout the Scriptures: while the term "forever" may sometimes be curtailed in duration by its context, such termination is never once mentioned in either the Old or New Testament as relating to the punishment of the wicked. Accordingly, the term continues to mean "everlasting" or "unending in its duration." Unfortunately, this is not recognized by those who are opposed to eternal punishment.
>
> Though the total testimony of the Old Testament is somewhat obscure on details, the main facts are clear. There is life after death. The life for the righteous is blessed; the life for the wicked is one of divine judgment and punishment. There is no intimation that this punishment should not be taken literally and continue eternally. Obviously, however, much additional light is cast upon the subject in the New Testament, where the word *hades* is equivalent to the Old Testament word *sheol*.[21]

The New Testament teaching by Walvoord on hell is extensive and includes the Greek words used in the New Testament and the teaching of Jesus on the subject. He supports his view on the eternality of hell's punishment with a large number of Scripture passages. His conclusion is very emphatic: "Scripture never challenges the concept that eternal punishment

---

21 Ibid., p. 18.

is by literal fire. Objections have to be on philosophic or theological grounds rather than on exegetical ones."[22]

Second, there are those who hold to the metaphorical view of hell set forth by William Crockett. It is far less specific than the orthodox view and less literal in its interpretation of Scripture.

Third, is the Roman Catholic view, set forth by Zachary Hayes. It is called the purgatorial view. This view is based upon an allegorical interpretation of Scripture. Roman Catholic clergy also depend on the apocryphal literature in order to support their view. There is no passage of Scripture which supports this view.

Fourth, some hold that hell is a temporary conditional time because they believe a literal hell view is in conflict with God's love and grace. This view is held by Clark H. Pinnock.

From a Biblical point of view, we must discover what God's Word teaches about this issue. All four views cannot all be correct. We should believe only in what Scripture teaches.

I personally believe that the orthodox view, as defended by Walvoord, is the view that the Bible sets forth.

HELL IN THE OLD TESTAMENT

There are several passages of Scripture in the Old Testament that are often used to support the doctrine of eternal punishment for those who have never accepted Christ as their personal Savior. These passages are Isaiah 66:22-24; Isaiah 14:9-11 and Daniel 12:1-3. I believe Isaiah 66:22-24 is the strongest of them:

> For as the new heavens and the new earth, which I will make, shall remain before me, saith the LORD, so shall your seed and your name remain. And it shall come to pass, that from one new moon to an-

---

22   Ibid., p. 28.

other, and from one sabbath to another, shall all flesh come to worship before me, saith the LORD. And they shall go forth, and look upon the carcases of the men that have transgressed against me: for their worm shall not die, neither shall their fire be quenched; and they shall be an abhorring unto all flesh.

The Ryrie Study Bible adds this note for these verses:

> "Like the eternal *new heavens* and *new earth*, Israel will endure forever (v. 22), *all flesh* will bow before the Lord forever (v. 23), and the wicked will be punished forever (v. 24)"[23]

I suspect many of us have heard multiple people say the word *hell*. A lot of people use the word regularly to emphasize their certainty about something or someone. I am sure those who use the word in this way do not even think about what the Bible teaches about hell or about the occupants who will be in that place and why they will go there.

But God's Word has a lot to say about both heaven and hell. We have already set forth what the Bible says about heaven. Now, we need to see what that same sacred book says about hell. The truth is that it has much to say about the eternal fire of hell. Of course, the fire of hell is not ignited with matches like Ohio Blue Tip or Diamond GreenLight. Instead, the eternal fire of hell—created by God—will forever torment anyone who has not received God's gift of salvation and His Son, the Lord Jesus Christ, as their Savior.

HELL IN THE NEW TESTAMENT

Two different Greek words are used in the New Testament to describe life after death for those outside of Christ. These terms are *hades* and *gehenna*. The strongest of the two is *gehenna*. It is translated as *hell* in

23 Charles Caldwell Ryrie, *Ryrie Study Bible Expanded Edition, New American Standard Bible* (Chicago: Moody Bible Institute, 1995), p. 1,147.

the New Testament, and it clearly refers to eternal punishment. Here are Biblical references in which this is true: Matthew 5:22, 29, 30; 10:28; 18:9; 23:15, 33; Mark 9:43, 45, 47; Luke 12:5; and James 3:6.

Jesus did teach that the degree of punishment in hell would not be the same for all who are there. This reality is illustrated in passages like Luke 12:47-48 and Mark 12:40. Clearly, He taught that there would be eternal punishment for the unregenerate. He said they would be cast into "the fire that never shall be quenched" (Mark 9:43).

Paul the apostle put it this way: "For God hath not appointed us to wrath, but to obtain salvation by our Lord Jesus Christ" (1 Thess. 5:9). He went on to say that these "shall be punished with everlasting destruction from the presence of the Lord, and from the glory of his power" (2 Thess. 1:9).

In the New Testament, the Greek term *aionios* is used to refer to an endless time or eternity.

Harry Buis described it this way:

> *Aionios* is used in the New Testament sixty times, fifty-one times of the happiness of the righteous, two times of the duration of God in His glory, six other times there is no doubt as to its meaning being endless, and seven times of the punishment of the wicked.[24]

Two other Biblical scholars state:

> This brief overview clearly demonstrates that the future punishment of the wicked in hell is a significant theme in the New Testament. It is woven into the whole fabric of New Testament teaching. In fact, future punishment is addressed in some way by *every* New Testament author. Matthew, Mark, Luke, John, Paul, James, Peter, Jude, and the unknown author of Hebrews *all* mention it in their writings. That could not be said of many important biblical truths.
>
> Another observation to be drawn from this overview is that the New

---

24 Harry Buis, *The Doctrine of Eternal Punishment* (Philadelphia, PA: Presbyterian and Reformed Publishing Company, 1957), p. 49.

Testament teaching concerning hell is somewhat diverse. At times, the pictures of hell even seem irreconcilable. How can burning fire coexist with the blackest darkness, for example? How can someone experience intense torment and yet perish? These presentations of hell should not be viewed as contradictory, however. Instead, they are better understood as complementary. Similar to the way in which different artists highlight varied characteristics of their particular subject, different depictions of hell bring out various shades that a monochromatic rendering could not.

Yet it should be noted that these different depictions of hell did not emerge as one might expect. It would seem plausible to expect that Matthew might focus on one aspect of hell, Mark another, Luke another, and even John another. In some ways, this is correct. Paul incorporates wrath into his doctrine of hell more than the others. James and Peter seem to place more stress on the destruction or death of the wicked. And Matthew places hell in contrast with the kingdom.

But an interesting thing to notice is that overall each New Testament writer's descriptions closely resemble those of the others. In fact, the diverse portraits of hell often come from the *same* biblical writer. Of course, it would be unwise to suppose that we could discover a detailed theology of hell in the brief excerpts on the subject by Mark, Luke, James, Peter, Jude, or the author of Hebrews. . . . But it is fascinating that similar pictures of hell emerge throughout the New Testament.[25]

A word of warning is in order. I strongly suggest that whenever we write, speak or teach about heaven or hell, we need to be sure not to isolate the one from the other. Both of these realities are taught in Scripture. We must not stress the one without stressing the other one. Remember, both of these are a part of the gospel message we share.

---

25 Christopher W. Morgan and Robert A. Peterson, general eds. *Hell Under Fire* (Grand Rapids: Zondervan, 2004), p. 142.

PART 3

WHAT ABOUT SUICIDE?

———————◆◆◆———————

Webster's New World Dictionary defines suicide as "the act of killing one's self on purpose," "harm or ruin suffered through one's own action," "a person who commits suicide."

News about suicide is on the rise. On Dec. 20, 2016, the *Dallas Morning News* carried an article by Seema Yasmin entitled "Does Suicide Rise During the Holidays?" Her answer to her own question is, "No, suicides don't increase over the holidays." She considers it a myth to believe otherwise. In the United States, suicide rates have increased according to the Center of Health Statistics. In fact, Yasmin states, "Suicide deaths are now the tenth leading cause of death across all ages and the fifth leading cause among people 15 to 24." Even among children, suicide rates have doubled since 2007.

Before seeking to answer the question of "Does the Bible condemn or condone suicide?", we should remember that the Bible does record evidence that some people did commit suicide.

Some examples of this can be found in the Old Testament. For instance, Saul and his armor-bearer took their own lives (1 Sam. 31:4-6).

Samuel records how Ahithophel hanged himself (2 Sam. 17:23). Zimri also acted in a similar way:

> And it came to pass, when Zimri saw that the city was taken, that he went into the palace of the king's house, and burnt the king's house over him with fire, and died.

Samson died along with the Philistines when he pulled the pillars down and killed himself and others (Judg. 16:28-31). And do not forget Abimelech, who also called his armor bearer and told him to use his sword to kill him (Judg. 9:54).

The New Testament also records how Judas the betrayer:

> ". . . when he saw that he was condemned, [he] repented himself, and brought again the thirty pieces of silver to the chief priests and elders, . . . and went and hanged himself. (Matt. 27:3-5)"[26]

For Bible-believing Christians the question is, What does the Bible teach about suicides?

James T. Clemons puts it this way:

> A wide variety of biblical texts have been used both to condemn and to condone the acts of suicide and attempted suicide.[27]

He cites examples that appear to teach about both of these views.

Now, suppose your loved one is told by doctors that they have done all they can do to help this person. They state that drugs can prolong life but cannot cure the problem. Your loved one says he or she accepts the doctors' verdict and wants to die and go to heaven.

Would it actually be cruel to try to prolong life in this case? On the other hand, could we, in fact, be assisting in the death of this individual if we did not?

---

26 For a fuller treatment of these Old and New Testament instances I recommend James T. Clemons, *What Does the Bible Say About Suicide?* (Minneapolis: Augsburg Fortress, 1990).

27 James T. Clemons, What Does the Bible Say About Suicide? (Minneapolis: Augsburg Fortress, 1990), pp. 51-72.

What does the Bible say about taking one's physical life? Does God's Word give us a definitive answer to these questions? The Bible does not speak directly and specifically about all the possibilities raised by this issue. However, it does tell us that God is the One who created man, and, therefore, it would seem that He should be the only one to end life.

Clemons cites the Hebrew Scriptures that deal with suicide or attempted suicide. These passages are 2 Samuel 1:1-16; 17:23; 1 Kings 16:18-19; Judges 9:52-54; 16:28-31; Jonah 1–4. In the New Testament he deals with Judas in Matthew 27:3-5 and with the Philippian jailer in Acts 16:19-34.[28]

I would encourage you to read these Scriptures carefully with a view toward understanding that God, the originator of life, is the only one who can rightfully take (or prescribe the taking of) that life.

Certainly, there is no Scriptural evidence to suggest that a true believer in Christ who commits suicide is in danger of losing his or her salvation (cf. John 10:28-29), and this may be a comfort to the friends and relatives of any person who has died in this horrible manner. However, neither is there any encouragement ever given for anyone to take his or her own life.

While there are many complex questions that may arise out of end-of-life situations related to medical care, the bottom line for the Christian is that we are prohibited from performing any deed that involves actively taking life from anyone—including ourselves. God alone has the prerogative of determining and overseeing the line between life and death (James 2:26).

---

28 All of these passages are explained carefully in James T. Clemons, *What Does the Bible Say About Suicide?* (Minneapolis: Augsburg Fortress, 1990), pp. 16-24.

PART 4

WHAT ABOUT GOD'S FUTURE JUDGMENTS?

—————◆◆◆—————

There are three specific future Divine judgments recorded in the Bible.

THE JUDGMENT SEAT OF CHRIST

Two major passages of Scripture speak of the judgement seat of Christ. The first one is 2 Corinthians 5:10, which states, "For we must all appear before the judgment seat of Christ; that every one may receive the things *done* in *his* body, according to that he hath done, whether *it be* good or bad."

The second passage is from Romans 14:10, where the text calls this the "judgment seat of Christ." This is referring to the same judgment as in 2 Corinthians 5:10.

The judgment seat in both of these texts according to Joseph Henry Thayer is:

> . . . a raised platform mounted by steps, a platform, tribute, used of the official seat of a judge . . . the structure, resembling a throne, which

Herod built in the theatre at Caesarea and from which he used to view the games and make speeches to the people.[29]

This judgment seat will appear when the Lord Jesus appears and believers will be present with Christ in the heavens. Believers will not appear at this judgment to determine whether or not they will go to heaven. Rather, they will be rewarded in accordance with their service for the Lord after they came to know Him as their personal Savior. The result of their presence there will reveal whether they will receive or lose a reward.[30]

In the following paragraphs, Dr. J. Dwight Pentecost has given us an excellent summary of the important aspects of the judgment seat of Christ:

> The time and place where this judgment seat of Christ will occur will be after believers will be caught up to meet the Lord in the air (1 Thess. 4:17), in other words, to be present with the Lord.

> The Judge will be none other than God the Son because the Father has given Him to be the judge since He has full divine authority for judgment (Rom. 14:10). The subjects of the judgment seat of Christ will be only believers. "There can be little doubt that the *bema* of Christ is concerned with believers. The first personal pronoun occurs with too great frequency in 2 Corinthians 5:1-19 to miss that point. Only the believer could have 'a house not made with hands, eternal in the heavens.' Only the believer could experience the working of God 'who also hath given unto us the earnest of the Spirit.' Only the believer could have the confidence that 'whilst we are at home in the body, we are absent from the Lord.' Only the believer could 'walk by faith, not by sight'(2 Cor. 5:6-7)."

> The result of the judgment seat of Christ at this time will be twofold, rewards received or rewards lost. That is, some who appear at this judgment will receive rewards based on their service for God. Remember,

---

29 Joseph Henry Thayer, *Greek-English Lexicon of the New Testament* (Findlay, OH: Dunham Publishing Co.), pp. 321-23.

30 For further information about this judgment see Tim Lahaye and Ed Hindson, *The Popular Encyclopedia of Bible Prophecy* (Eugene, OR: Harvest House Publishers, 2004), pp. 182-83.

this is not the Great White Throne judgment but it is the judgment seat of Christ which has to do with those who are believers. But those believers who have not been faithful in their service for God will lose rewards (2 Cor. 3:13).[31]

THE GREAT WHITE THRONE JUDGMENT

Scripture tells us that the great white throne judgment will be after the 1,000-year reign of Christ on the earth (Rev. 20:1-5). It also appears that this judgment takes place somewhere between heaven and earth, based on Revelation 20:11. The people involved in this judgment are described as "the rest of the dead" (Rev. 20:5). Apparently, these words refer to all the unsaved dead because they are the only ones who are yet to be resurrected.

The *Ryrie Study Bible* note on Revelation 20:5 is helpful in understanding this verse:

> *The rest of the dead.* The wicked dead will be raised and judged after the Millennium. *The first resurrection* refers back to the end of verse 4. This resurrection includes all the righteous (the resurrection of life, John 5:29, and the resurrection of the just, Luke 14:14), who will be raised before the Millennium begins. [32]

This is the final dreaded judgment. All the unsaved of all ages will appear at this judgment. It is described in Revelation 20:11-15. Jesus sits upon this throne. And His appearance is fearsome—so much so that heaven and earth flee from before Him. And with good reason, for all who appear before this throne will be condemned to spend eternity consciously suffering in the lake of fire.

---

31 See J. Dwight Pentecost, *Things to Come* (Findlay, OH: Dunham Publishing House, 1958), pp. 219-23.

32 Charles Caldwell Ryrie, *Ryrie Study Bible Expanded Edition. New American Standard Bible* (Chicago: Moody Press, 1995), p. 2,041.

As each person appears before the Lord Jesus, a series of books is reviewed in which their deeds have been recorded. One book in particular stands out–it is the book of life. Because "there is none righteous, no, not one" (Rom. 3:10), every person who stands before Christ will find that their works are inadequate, and–having failed to trust Him–their names will not be found in the book of life.

In my summary of the great white throne judgment, I want to set forth three questions often asked by people about this judgment and give my answers.

Will the unsaved suffer eternally?

Yes, they will suffer in what the Bible calls "the lake of fire" (Rev. 20:14). Conscious, eternal torment awaits those who have not trusted Christ as their Savior. He Himself said those not rightly related to Him would "go away into everlasting punishment" (Matt. 25:46).

I believe that whatever heaven is, hell is the opposite. Those who are ushered into heaven will dwell there forever. Conversely, those who are consigned to the lake of fire will be there forever. There are degrees of reward for those who dwell in heaven, and I believe that there will be degrees of punishment for those in hell. I believe that Jesus lends credence to this as he sums up the parable of the faithful steward:

> And that servant, which knew his lord's will, and prepared not *himself*, neither did according to his will, shall be beaten with many *stripes*. But he that knew not, and did commit things worthy of stripes, shall be beaten with few *stripes*. For unto whomsoever much is given, of him shall be much required; and to whom men have committed much, of him they will ask the more. (Luke 12:47-48)

Thus, some person in a remote location who never heard the gospel would be consigned to the lake of fire, but that person's punishment would not be as severe as, say, a person who has committed such egregious acts as Adolf Hitler.

Are the flames in hell literal?

The punishment is real and is felt by the person being punished. If the flames are not literal, the result of being engulfed in them will be worse than physical fire. But once again, if the plain sense makes literal sense, seek no other sense. Flames are used to describe the punishment in every passage that describes hell or punishment in the afterlife. There is no reason not to understand these flames of hell to be literal. Therefore, the flames are probably literal, and the torment of those in hell is *definitely* literal.

How can hell be outer darkness if there is eternal fire?

The Bible says both things are true. Some people also question how hell can be a lake (associated with water, which extinguishes flame) of fire. But even here on earth, most of us will remember images from the Gulf War of pools of crude oil boiling with flame. Some liquids burn quite intensely, and in the case of hell, they do so eternally.

The *fire* of hell may not dispense light, but it will be just as painful. And that is the important thing to remember. Whatever it is, hell is a place to be avoided at all cost. No sacrifice on our part is too great or too small to spread the everlasting gospel. Hell *is* real–and we need to be on a dead run to depopulate it.

THE JUDGMENT OF SATAN AND WICKED ANGELS

In Scripture, we are not given the specific place where the judgment of Satan and his wicked angels will be fulfilled. It will most likely take place in the angelic realm.

The Apostle Peter told us that God has sent some of the demons or wicked angels into "hell, and delivered *them* into chains of darkness, to be reserved unto judgment" (2 Pet. 2:4).

We might ask also, "What is the basis for this judgment?" Based on two passages of Scripture, we can say the angels will be judged in this way because they followed Satan when he said, "I will ascend into heaven, I will exalt my throne above the stars of God: I will sit also upon the mount of the congregation, in the sides of the north: I will ascend above the heights of the clouds; I will be like the most High" (Isa. 14:13-14).

Notice the five "I wills" in this passage.

The second passage which tells us about the basis on which Satan will be judged is in Ezekiel 28:12-19. Here, as in the Isaiah 14 passage, the prophet was led by the Spirit of God to tell us that the basis for the judgment of Satan was because he desired to be like God; his "heart was lifted up because of [his] beauty" (v. 17) and because of "the multitude of [his] iniquities" (v. 18).

Also, the Apostle John tells us in Revelation 20:10 that "the devil that deceived them was cast into the lake of fire and brimstone, where the beast and the false prophet *are*, and shall be tormented day and night for ever and ever."

PART 5

WHERE WILL YOU SPEND ETERNITY?

◆◆◆

S urely, if you have read this far, you have been thinking about where you will spend eternity. That is good. I truly hope you have decided that you do not want to go to the hell described in this book. If you have, I believe God has led you to that decision. Of course, believing you do not want to go to hell does not bring you to the certainty of going to heaven. God has given us His Word in the Bible so that we can know how to be sure of our salvation, which is our certainty of going to heaven when we die.

GOD'S PLAN OF SALVATION

Salvation is from the Lord. It is His work from start to finish. The writer of Hebrews described this marvelous undertaking, which is all from God, as a "great salvation" (Heb. 2:3). There simply is no greater or more wonderful accomplishment man could ever experience. Salvation from sin is God's work on behalf of humans alone. No other creatures experience God's salvation. In contrast to humans, God's grace was not extended to those angelic beings who followed Satan in his rebellion, as we have seen.

The Bible presents an ugly picture of man as sinner. All sinned in Adam. All received a sinful nature or disposition from their parents and all commit deeds of sin very early in life. All are without God and without hope. The unregenerate rebel against the idea of their inability to make some contribution to their eternal welfare. Even the regenerate often chafe at the thought of presenting the gospel as God's grace plus absolutely nothing. "Results" seem to come much easier and faster and—today—are said to be more genuine, if we allow the sinner even an infinitesimally small part in his salvation. But Scripture will not support such a view. It views all humans in the same way—without any merit before a holy God and, therefore, unable to make any contribution toward their salvation.

Three major themes occupy our attention in this section—the demand for the plan, the Designer of the plan and the development of the plan.

The demand for the plan

Guilty sinners, dead in trespasses and sin and without any merit before God, will not and cannot initiate contact with God. God must make the first move if ever He and wayward sinners are to be reunited.

And He has initiated a plan to bring sinners back to Himself. Both Scripture and reason argue for the divine plan of salvation. To disbelieve this is to dishonor the all-wise God.

God is a God of design and order. He is also a God of justice. He created man in His image to enjoy His fellowship. But man sinned. If the sinner is to ever be restored to a right relationship with God, God must devise a plan of salvation, and, thankfully, He has done so. If we may say it reverently, God had a problem and He solved it.

Man's sin not only affected him; it affected God, too. All sin affects

God. We observed earlier how sin made its mark upon Adam and Eve and, through them, upon the whole human race. Very severe penalties were inflicted upon the sinners in the garden, upon the serpent and even upon the ground because of mans' sin. The question remains, What relationship, if any, did Adam's sin and our sin in him have upon God?

Sin is an offense against God. He is the norm, the standard, the criterion of judging right from wrong. Therefore, sin is an offense against His holy character. Sin did not surprise God or intrude into His universe unnoticed.

God's ineffable purity cannot tolerate sin. He is "of purer eyes than to behold evil" (Hab. 1:13). How, then, can man ever come before Him? How can God "be just, and the justifier of him which believeth in Jesus" (Rom. 3:26)?

God is righteous and always deals righteously with the sinner. The solution is in Christ's cross. It was here that God's love was poured out, and at the same time, all His just demands were met. God solved the problem of man's sin presented to Him. He is the only one who could.

After man's fall, God the Father began in time the plan of salvation that He ordained in eternity past. This divine plan centered in His Divine Son; "He gave his only begotten Son" because He "so loved the world" (John 3:16), and His Son "laid down his life for us" (1 John 3:16).

From the time God clothed Adam and Eve with the skins of the slain animals, the great program of redemption through blood had begun. Genesis 3:15 in particular anticipates the coming of the Seed of the woman who was to inflict a fatal wound upon Satan: "it shall bruise thy head." This Seed was none other than Jesus Christ the Messiah. The sacrifices of the Old Testament were types of Him Who was to come—God clothed in human flesh to become the substitute for every member of Adam's lost race.

In the Divine solution, Christ was the righteous One Who alone could satisfy every demand of the offended righteousness of God. The cross of Christ is presented in Holy Scripture as the declaration of the very righteousness of God (Rom. 3:25). Through that cross, "God was in Christ, reconciling the world unto Himself" (2 Cor. 5:19).

Since Calvary, the question before lost humans is not one concerned primarily with their original sin. It is now a question of what they will do with Christ the Son who died for them. There is only one condition they must meet in order to be made right with God.

The Divine plan of salvation, formulated in eternity past, allowed for the entrance and continuance of sin until the day appointed by God when sin and its author shall be banished forever.

In his sermon on the day of Pentecost, Peter, described Christ and His accusers:

> . . . being delivered by the determinate counsel and foreknowledge of God, ye have taken, and by wicked hands have crucified and slain. (Acts 2:23).

On another occasion as Peter and John preached, it was said that those who had gathered to crucify Christ were doing "whatsoever thy hand and thy counsel determined before to be done" (Acts 4:27-28). The same apostle also said Christ "was foreordained before the foundation of the world, but was manifest in these last times for you" (1 Pet. 1:20).

If the historic death of Christ was a part of the Divine plan as the solution to the sin question, then the entrance of sin which made that death necessary was also known and permitted.

The Designer of the plan

Each of the three members of the holy Trinity—the Father, Son, and Holy Spirit—has a vital part in man's salvation. The three are referred to in relation to man's salvation in the first chapter of Ephesians. The Father and the Son are highlighted in the first 12 verses, and the Spirit is discussed in verses 13 and 14.

The Father "hath chosen us" (Eph. 1:4) in Christ and "predestined us" (v. 5). All of this is "to the good pleasure of His will" (v. 5) and "to the praise of the glory of His grace" (v. 6). He is the One who has accepted us "in the beloved" (v. 6).

The Son is the beloved One "in whom we have redemption" and "forgiveness of sins" (v 7).

The Spirit seals the believer (v. 13) and "is the earnest of our inheritance" (v. 14).

Throughout Scripture, various roles related to man's salvation are ascribed to the different persons of the Godhead.

There is a danger of compartmentalizing the redemptive work of the members of the Godhead. This usually occurs when the Father's love of sinners is emphasized. The implication often left in doing this is that the Son came because it was His Father's will, and not because He, too, loves sinners.

There is complete harmony among the members of the Trinity. While each one has specific roles (i.e., the Son died, not the Father), there is always concurrence and mutual involvement in what is done. There is a subordination of office but not a subordination of essence.

The complex miracle of physical birth requires a Divine plan and planner. This is even more true of the miracle of spiritual birth into the family of God. The Author of the plan of redemption is none other than God Himself. The Creator of the universe and of man who spoke and brought all things into existence deigned to devise a plan of salvation for His disobedient and fallen creatures. God the Father's love and grace is displayed beautifully and abundantly in His plan of salvation.

John declared that those who receive Christ as Savior are the recipients of the very power of God and, in fact, are born of God (John 1:12-13).

We are told by Paul that Christ, the Savior, is "the wisdom of God" (1 Cor. 1:24; cf. v. 30). Paul also reminds us that it was God the Father who displayed His Son publicly as a propitiation, or satisfaction, for man's sin. It was through the work on the cross by the Savior that the Father could remain just and at the same time justify all who believe in Christ as Savior (Rom. 3:25-26).

Salvation must never be viewed as an afterthought or as the only possible way out of a hopeless dilemma which God faced. Just like God Himself, the great plan of salvation is eternal and orderly.

God was certainly not shocked when Adam and Eve sinned and plunged the whole human race into sin, guilt, and degradation. Every possible human instrument in the plan of salvation is eliminated. John the apostle said it was not of blood (not of human lineage), nor of the will of the flesh, nor of the will or desire of man (John 1:13). No, it is all of God. It is His plan from start to finish. Salvation is indeed of the Lord.

The development of the plan

The plan of redemption, which the Father designed in eternity past before He even created man, has been realized in time. In His infinite wisdom, God solved the problem man's sin caused. His solution involved the choice of sinful humans on whom He would bestow His grace and salvation.

The foundation of God's plan of salvation is His justice, holiness, mercy, and grace. God's holiness means He possesses absolute perfection in every detail and is completely separate from evil, both in His person and in His relationships with sinners. To say God is righteous and just is to speak of His holiness as He relates to His creatures—humans. God's own nature is His standard to which He demands conformity.

God never violates His holiness and neither does He allow His creatures to violate it without full payment and satisfaction. That is what

Scripture means when it ascribes justice to God.

The grace of God has to do with the undeserved favor He displays toward sinners. His mercy is His withholding of merited judgment. The Author of the plan of salvation is the God of love, holiness, justice, mercy, and grace.

We often feel that everything about our salvation began when we made our decision to trust Christ as Savior. The fact is, God was at work on our behalf long before that moment of decision. We did not—we could not—initiate the salvation we enjoy in Christ.

Scripture declares that we were chosen in Christ "before the foundation of the world" (Eph. 1:4). Peter told the scattered Christians they were chosen "according to the foreknowledge of God the Father" (1 Pet. 1:1-2).

Paul, the apostle to the Gentiles, put it this way:

> For whom he did foreknow, he also did predestinate *to be* conformed to the image of His Son (Rom. 8:29).

And again we read,

> God hath from the beginning chosen you to salvation through sanctification of the Spirit and belief of the truth" (2 Thess. 2:13).

The Savior Himself spoke of the sovereign, electing work of God the Father to the multitudes who came to Him to hear Him:

> All that the Father giveth me shall come to me; and him that cometh to me I will in no wise cast out. No man can come to me, except the Father which hath sent me draw him: and I will raise him up at the last day (John 6:37, 44).

We do not understand why God has been pleased to do the things He has. Why were we chosen and brought to faith in Christ when many others were not? Why were many called but only a few chosen (Matt.

22:14)? We will never know the answers to many of our queries until we see the Savior face to face. There is one thing we do know, however. We know that God's plan is the best possible plan to bring the most possible glory now and eternally to His name. It is our knowledge of Him from His Word that tells us this plan.

Evangelical Christians who take seriously the Scriptural teaching on election are divided over how it should be understood. There are basically three viewpoints on this important doctrine.

Some believe God has elected sinners to be saved on the basis of the faith that He knew they would one day have. God "chose those who He foreknew would accept Christ."[33] This is a popular explanation among those Christians who think about election. The major weakness of this interpretation is that it seems to view God's foreknowledge merely as foresight.

A second view that might be called corporate or group election is another view that is becoming quite popular. The idea here is of God's election of the church in Christ rather than individuals being elected before the foundation of the world. Those who believe in Christ become a part of the elect group and can therefore be called elect ones.

A contemporary spokesman for this view stated it this way:

> Christ is the chosen One in and through whom in corporate solidarity with Him the church is selected to be God's own. No one is ever chosen *on his own,* that is, outside of Christ, or apart from incorporation into the church.[34]

The major weakness with this view is its failure to deal adequately with those Scriptures which relate election to individuals.

Among four and five-point Calvinists, election is understood to be:

---

33 Henry Clarence Thiessen, *Introductory Lectures in Systematic Theology* (Grand Rapids: Eerdmans Publishing Co., 1949), p. 344.

34 Clark H. Pinnock, gen. ed., *The Grace of God, the Will of Man* (Grand Rapids: Zondervan Publishing Co., 1989), p. 228.

That eternal act of God whereby He, in His sovereign good pleasure, and on account of no foreseen merit in them, chooses a certain number of men to be the recipients of special grace and of eternal salvation.[35]

Those who hold to this view often fail to take into account the fact that Scripture does sometimes speak of what might be called group election—the church—in addition to individual election. Also, Scripture does involve God's foreknowledge in His election (cf. 1 Pet. 1:1-2).

It seems most in harmony with the totality of Scripture to believe in personal, pre-temporal election as well as a corporate election of the church. God's foreknowledge of human faith in His election both of individuals and the church must also be included. He did predestine those whom He foreknew (Rom. 8:29). And He did choose according to His foreknowledge (1 Pet. 1:1-2). We are not told what it was in God's foreknowledge which moved Him to choose. It is going beyond what Scripture says to say it was His knowledge of the sinner's faith which caused Him to make the choice.

The precious truths of election and salvation will not make one self-absorbed, or unconcerned for the lost, if rightly understood and balanced with God's commands involving human responsibilities. His plan is the result of His infinite wisdom and love and is in line with His absolute holiness justice, mercy, and grace.

The eternal plan of salvation includes not only the end—a redeemed company in glory—but the means to the end, as well. And it includes a holy, loving, and intelligent being behind it. These things contrast this plan with fatalism, which does not include the means, nor does it have an intelligent being behind it.

Scripture does not present God's plan as incompatible with man's will. The sovereign plan includes the actions and responsibilities of men. It is all part of His plan.

---

35 L. Berkhof, *Systematic Theology* (Grand Rapids: Eerdmans Publishing Co ., 1941), p. 114. Italics in original.

Paul associated the matter of his call to salvation with his responsibility to serve Christ (Gal. 1:15-16). God's choice of us becomes the motivating force for our service to Him. These truths concerning our salvation ought to humble us.

A proper understanding of these glorious truths will bring us where Paul was brought after his long discourse on the subject. His hymn of praise should be made our own:

> O the depth of the riches both of the wisdom and knowledge of God! how unsearchable *are* his judgments, and his ways past finding out!

> For who hath known the mind of the Lord? or who hath been his counsellor? Or who hath first given to Him, and it shall be recompensed unto Him again? For of Him, and through Him, and to Him, *are* all things: to whom *be* glory for ever. Amen. (Rom. 11:33-36)

THE HOLY SPIRIT'S ROLE IN SALVATION

Apart from the Father's work there would have been no plan of salvation. Without the Son's work there would have been no provision of salvation, as we have already seen. Apart from the Spirit's work there would be no application of this great salvation to man's needs. It is the third member of the Godhead who procures salvation for all who believe. He applies the finished work of Christ to the believing sinner who was chosen by God.

There are two major works of the Holy Spirit in man's salvation: His general work upon the unregenerate and His specific work in salvation.

His general work

The Spirit's general work is His ministry upon all people everywhere, without distinction of their knowledge, spiritual experience or relationship to God.

Charles Hodge defined this work of the Spirit:

> The Holy Spirit, as the Spirit of truth, of holiness and of life in all its forms is present with every human mind enforcing truth, restraining from evil, exciting to good, and imparting wisdom or strength when, where, and in what measure seemeth to Him good . . . this is what in theology is called common grace.[36]

Referring to the work of the Spirit as *grace* does not mean that it provides the sinner with abilities or capabilities that would enable him to move toward the Savior. It certainly does not mean that because of this work of the Spirit man can now make some contribution—add his part—to his salvation. The general work of the Spirit upon the unregenerate, which is also known as *common grace*, simply refers to God's undeserved favor displayed toward all.

Three things explain the reality and need for this precious activity of the Spirit.

First, God's sovereignty and providence imply such a ministry. Since He is the supreme ruler, sustainer and preserver of life, it follows naturally that He would exhibit such an attitude toward His creatures.

Second, this work of the Spirit is absolutely essential since man is the sinner he is. On his own, the *natural* or unregenerate person cannot receive spiritual truth (1 Cor. 2:14). To him, the gospel is *foolishness* (1 Cor. 1:18). In other words, apart from the work of the Spirit, the unregenerate have no hope whatsoever.

Third, mankind could not survive the results of his own sinfulness and Satan's power were it not for the restraining work of the Spirit of God. Satan's power and wickedness demand a Divine power to counter and supersede it. The Holy Spirit is that power. He holds back the full onslaught of wickedness in this world and will continue to do so until the Divinely appointed time.

---

36 Charles Hodge, *Systematic Theology* (Grand Rapids: Eerdmans Publishing Co., 1968), 2:667.

There are three specific activities the Holy Spirit performs which illustrate His general work on the unregenerate.

The most general of these activities is His providential care over His creatures. The Spirit of God has compassion on all and showers many natural blessings upon them universally. The rain and sunshine, for example, come to the just and to the unjust. The laws of nature (i.e., seed time and harvest) hold true for all. Both the Old and New Testaments make this clear (i.e., Ps. 145:9; Matt. 5:45; Luke 6:35; Acts 14:17).

A second illustration of the general work of the Holy Spirit upon the unregenerate involves His restraint of sin.

The term "strive" in Genesis 6:3 means that the Spirit *holds back*. He restrains sin in the world. An example of this is when God kept Satan from having total control over Job (cf. Job 1:12). He restrained sin. Paul wrote to the Thessalonian believers about one "who now letteth" (2 Thess. 2:7). While interpreters differ over who this one is, it seems certain to be the Holy Spirit since He is the restrainer of sin in the Old Testament. Furthermore, He is in the immediate context and is a member of the Godhead, which would be required in order to withstand Satan to such a degree.

The Holy Spirit's conviction of sin is the third illustration of His work of common grace. Jesus said the Spirit He would send would "reprove the world of sin, and of righteousness, and of judgment" (John 16:8). This means the Holy Spirit would give demonstrable proof of the truth of the gospel message. Humans are in a state of sin (note the singular "sin" in John 16:8) because they do not believe in Christ. The Spirit proves that Christ is righteous because He rose from the dead and returned to the Father. The Spirit also proves that judgment is sure to come because it has come in the past through the judgment of Satan at the cross.

In this way, the Holy Spirit enlightens the minds of the unsaved, who are blinded by Satan (2 Cor. 4:4). Not all who are thus enlightened respond in faith, however. This work by itself is not sufficient for salvation, but it does provide the sinner with proof of the truthfulness of the gospel message. If and when that message is received, the Spirit's work of giving life becomes operative.

How, we might ask, does the Spirit do these things where the gospel has not been taken? We are not told. Perhaps in such cases, God the Spirit performs this work through God's revelation of Himself in nature and in man's conscience. Some attempt to solve this problem by restricting the meaning of the *world* in John 3:16 to the world of the elect. There does not seem to be any reason, however, in the text or context for doing this.

His specific work in salvation

All the general ministries of the Spirit with the unregenerate that we have discussed fall short of actual salvation. God did not intend that they should save. The general ministries of the Spirit do show man his need for salvation; they leave him without excuse before God. They are genuine ministries of God, but they precede the Spirit's saving work by preparing His way for salvation.

Salvation becomes a reality when, at the moment of faith, the Holy Spirit imparts life to the believing sinner. When the Holy Spirit moves in this way upon the individual, His ministry is always 100 percent effective (note in Rom. 8:28-30 that those *called* are *glorified*).

This work of the Spirit in moving sinners to trust in Christ, the sin-bearer, has been called *irresistible grace, efficacious grace* or *effectual grace*. All the other works of the Holy Spirit as previously described come before this saving work. They involve a process continuing over a period of time. However, that work of the Spirit which results in the individual's acceptance of Christ as Savior is not a process. Rather, it is an instantaneous act that is simultaneous with faith. Scriptural support for this effectual work of the Spirit is found in the following passages: Romans 1:1; 8:28; 1 Timothy 6:12; and 2 Peter 1:3, 10.

The work of the Spirit that accomplishes salvation produces regenera-tion. Though the word *regeneration* appears only twice in Scripture (Matt. 19:28; Titus 3:5), the concept of being *born again* occurs often (i.e., John 3:3). Regeneration means just that—to be *born again*. It has to do with the impartation of life from God to the sinner.

The means by which regeneration is accomplished eliminates all human endeavor. Though personal faith in Christ the Savior is necessary, faith does not produce the new life. Human faith and Divine regeneration occur at the same time, but one is man's responsibility as he is enabled by the Holy Spirit, and the other is the work of God imparting the Divine life.

The work of regeneration is ascribed to each member of the Godhead (e.g., John 5:21; Tit. 3:5; Js. 1:17-18). It is not based on experience, though the life of one who has been regenerated will surely be different. The results of this instantaneous sovereign work of the Spirit include a new nature (2 Cor. 5:17), new righteousness (Rom. 5:19), new life (e.g., John 3:9; 4:7; 5:1) and eternal life (Phil. 1:6).

There are many riches of God's grace which are a part of salvation. Here we want to consider only those which are the result of the Holy Spirit's work at the time of salvation.

First, the Spirit baptizes or identifies the believing sinner with Christ, the Head of the body, and with every other member of that body.

There is much confusion abroad today over this work of the Spirit. This confusion usually centers around two errors. One of these is to make Spirit baptism a ministry which comes after salvation. The other error relates to making speaking in tongues a sign of the baptism.[37]

These and many problems will be eliminated if the following truths are accepted.

The baptism of the Spirit is peculiar to the church age. It cannot be

---

37 See Robert Lightner, *Speaking in Tongues and Divine Healing* (Schaumburg, IL: Regular Baptist Press, 1978).

found in any other dispensation. Every reference to it in the gospels and even in Acts 1:5 is future. All believers of this dispensation are baptized by the Holy Spirit:

> For as the body is one, and hath many members, and all the members of that one body, being many, are one body: so also is Christ. For by one Spirit are we all baptized into one body, whether *we be* Jews or Gentiles, whether *we be* bond or free; and have been all made to drink into one Spirit (1 Cor. 12:12-13).

No command is ever given to be baptized by the Spirit. This s a Divine work which accompanies salvation, whereby the Holy Spirit identifies the believing sinner with Christ and His work (Rom. 6:1-10) and makes him a member of the body of Christ. Because of the tense used in 1 Corinthians 12:13, and since the work of the Spirit effects a union with Christ and His body, it is experienced only once by each believer. It cannot be repeated. This work of the Spirit is not based upon human experience or derived from it. This means the individual need not be conscious of it or experience some great emotional stir to be assured of it.

The baptism by the Spirit is not to be confused with the filling of the Spirit. This latter ministry is repeatable and involves human cooperation (cf. Acts 2:4; 4:31; see also Eph. 5:18, where the present tense is used to indicate continuous action). Neither is it true that all who were baptized with the Spirit spoke with tongues (See 1 Cor. 12:13 and compare with 1 Cor. 12:30).

Second, the Spirit indwells the people of God. He takes up residence in each and every believer (1 Cor. 6:19).

Third, the Spirit seals the sinner who trusts the Savior. At the same time as salvation and the two ministries listed above, the Holy Spirit seals the believing sinner. He is the seal (2 Cor. 1:22; Eph. 1:13; 4:30). This guarantee of eternal security is true of each and every believer. This spiritual ministry is performed at the time of salvation and without any human effort.

A threefold significance describes the intent of this sealing, according to Ryrie. First is "the certainty of possession by God." Second, there is "the certainty of the promise of His salvation, for there is no power greater than God who could break the seal, and God Himself has promised never to break it." Third, the seal gives us "the certainty of His purpose to keep us until the day of redemption."[38]

Two things need to be emphasized in relation to the Holy Spirit's role in salvation.

First, the general work of the Spirit upon the unregenerate should encourage the believer to share his faith with others. The Spirit is at work preparing the way. He is the only One who convicts and draws sinners to the Savior.

Second, the Spirit of God is the One who brings life to the sinner and who accomplishes all the other works enabling the child of God to live to the glory of God. These works of the Spirit are totally unrelated to human merit or accomplishment and are eternal in nature. The Holy Spirit's role in salvation empowers us to fruitful evangelism and enables the sinner to come to salvation.

THE HUMAN CONDITION
OF SALVATION

"What must I do to be saved?" the jailer at Philippi asked Paul and Silas (Acts 16:30). When you are lost, proper directions are very important. How terrible to give wrong directions to someone transporting a dying person to the hospital! How much more terrible to give sinners the wrong directions to heaven.

Although Scripture repeatedly declares that salvation is by faith alone, plus *nothing*, various conditions have been added to the gospel from time to

---

38 Charles C. Ryrie, *The Holy Spirit* (Chicago: Moody Press, 1965), pp. 81-82.

time in the history of the church. Some groups, even within evangelicalism, are known for their insistence on certain human actions or attitudes in addition to faith for salvation.

Today, the evangelical community is divided over whether Christ must be received as Lord of the sinner's life as well as Savior or substitute for sin. There is also a growing sympathy among evangelicals for what is called *Biblical universalism* and also for a form of annihilationism. We will address these issues in this section after we review the one condition of salvation clearly stated in Scripture.

The condition of salvation must be understood to apply to those who are mentally capable of meeting that condition.

How does God's great plan of salvation benefit the individual sinner? The Father planned everything. The Son of God, "the last Adam" (1 Cor. 15:45), gave Himself as a substitute for the descendants of the first Adam. The Spirit uses the Word of God to convict the sinner and draw him to the Savior. But what part does the sinner play in all of this? What must he or she do to be saved?

The condition in the present dispensation

The present dispensation[39] (a distinctive epoch of God's testing of man) refers to the time from the birth of the church until the rapture of the church. Dispensationalists are frequently wrongly accused of believing in a different way of salvation for each dispensation; however, dispensations involve testing, each one showing the necessity of God's one plan of salvation.

Personal faith in the Lord Jesus Christ alone as Savior is the one and only condition for human salvation. More than 100 times in the New Testament faith in Christ, for those who are capable of exercising it, is

39 See Charles C. Ryrie, *Dispensationalism Today* (Chicago: Moody Press, 1965), p. 29. Here dispensationalism is defined as "a distinguishable economy in the outworking of God's purpose."

made the one human requirement for receiving eternal life.

Lewis Sperry Chafer writes,

> There are one hundred and fifteen passages at least wherein the word *believe* is used alone and apart from every other condition as the only way of salvation. In addition to this there are upwards of 35 passages wherein its synonym *faith* is used.[40]

To be sure, there are essentials the sinner must know before he can be saved. He is a guilty sinner (Rom. 3:23); sin's wages is death (Rom. 6:23); Christ died in the sinner's place (Rom. 5:8; 1 Cor. 15:3); and the sinner must trust Christ alone as his sin-bearer (John 3:16; Acts 16:31). These are the essentials of the gospel. Yet mere knowledge of them does not bring about the new birth. Only at the point of personal reception and acceptance of Christ alone as Savior, by the drawing power of the Holy Spirit, does the guilty sinner pass from death unto life and into the family of God.

"Without faith *it is* impossible to please" God (Heb. 11:6). That is as true when it comes to salvation as it is in every other area, and yet it must be emphasized that it is not man's faith which saves him. Man's faith is not the cause of his salvation. It is Jesus Christ, the *object* of our faith, who saves us. Christ and Christ alone saves sinners; faith does not. Salvation, however, is always *through* faith by God's marvelous grace.

The gospel is sometimes presented as though some special kind or amount of faith is required for salvation. Satan often comes to the newborn child of God and brings doubts as to whether he had enough faith or has believed in the right way. As far as Scripture is concerned, God simply requires all the faith or trust one has and that one's faith be in Jesus Christ. The sinner's reception of God's great gift of salvation adds nothing to the completed work of Christ. Were that true, it would be Christ's substitutionary atonement plus faith in Christ which saves. Christ's work alone

---

40   Lewis Sperry Chafer, *Salvation* (Wheaton, IL: Van Kampen Press, 1917), p. 49.

saves, but unless His person and work are received by faith, no benefit comes to the individual sinner.

Man's faith must have the proper object before salvation results. God does not simply demand belief in the ultimate triumph of good, or faith in the evangelical church, or even faith in His own existence and power, as that which brings salvation. It is always faith in God's Son as the Divine substitute for sin which brings life to the spiritually dead sinner.

This involves Christ's death on the cross. According to Scripture there is an offense, a stigma, attached to the cross. God has done everything and man makes no contribution whatsoever to the finished work of Christ or to his own salvation. Paul indicated that the offense of the cross was the absence of human work from God's way of salvation (Gal. 5:11). Man desires to make some contribution, however small, but he cannot— "it is finished" (John 19:30). Faith in Christ is not a work. As stated by J. Gresham Machen, "Faith consists not in doing something but in receiving something."[41]

Think about getting a gift or giving a gift. A gift does not cease to be a gift just because the one to whom it is given receives it. Salvation is a gift—God's gift—and it remains a gift even after it is received by faith.

The person who is truly born again will want to serve Christ. Life cannot be hidden very long. Life ushers in growth. The growth evidences itself in service. Paul's exhortation to Titus is applicable to all believers. Every child of God must "be careful to maintain good works" (Tit. 3:8). This is not so that one might be saved or remain saved but rather because he *is* saved.

The condition in other dispensations

The Bible knows of only one way of salvation. It makes no difference which period of time one refers to. The salvation of a sinner has always been

---

41 J. Gresham Machen, *What Is Faith?* (Grand Rapids: Eerdmans Publishing Co., 1925), p. 172.

and will always be by God's grace through faith. The basis upon which God forgives sin has always been the substitutionary death of Christ. People have not always known what we know about the person and work of Christ simply because all that has been revealed in the New Testament was not made known to the men of God who wrote the Old Testament. Therefore, while God has always required personal faith as a condition of salvation, the complexity of that faith has not always been the same. Those who lived before Calvary knew very little about the finished work of Christ that is so vividly portrayed in the New Testament. Many of the Old Testament sacrifices and offerings were types of the Savior and of the final and complete work He would eventually do. However, even though the people may not have known all that was involved when they believed God and His promises, He accounted their faith to them for righteousness because He accepted the work of His Son as already finished. The resurrection of Christ is proof of this acceptance.

The only difference between other dispensations and this one, as it relates to salvation, is the complexity of the faith which was believed by the sinner. Before the full revelation of Scripture was given, faith was placed in the person and promises of God made known up to that time (Rom. 4:3). Since God has made known to man the meaning of the death of His Son, faith is now placed in His person and work. Salvation in any age is a work of God on behalf of the believing sinner, apart from human works of any kind.

Human additions to the one condition

Water baptism. Many people depend on ritual baptism, received either as infants or as adults, for their salvation. This is an entirely false hope. All the water in the world could not take away even one sin. Nowhere does Scripture make water baptism a condition for salvation. The Bible teaches that an obedient believer will obey the Lord and His Word and be baptized, identifying himself with a Bible-believing church.

Water baptism, however—symbolically, not literally—identifies one with Christ in His death, burial, and resurrection. Water baptism gives public demonstration to the fact that the believer has already been identified with Christ, having trusted Him as personal Savior.

Several passages of Scripture, taken by themselves, seem to include water baptism as a condition of salvation. The following are the major problem passages used by those who believe water baptism is essential for salvation.

A generally acknowledged rule of Bible interpretation is to arrive at a Biblical teaching based upon the clear and undisputed texts. Whatever problem texts that exist must then be viewed in relation to the clear ones. The difficult passages must not be ignored or twisted, or given an interpretation which will not stand up under rigorous scrutiny. Rather, the interpreter's obligation is to see if the problem passages will yield to an interpretation which is in harmony with the clear passages. If this cannot be done, the existing conflict between the clear texts and the problem ones must be allowed to stand until further light comes. The disputed text must not become dominant over the undisputed one. In other words, we do not build a doctrine on problematic texts and then adjust the clear ones to fit that doctrine. It is really the other way around.

Mark 16:15-16 states:

> And he said unto them, Go ye into all the world, and preach the gospel to every creature. He that believeth and is baptized shall be saved; but he that believeth not shall be damned.

This passage is included in a longer passage, Mark 16:9-20, which appears in the *Textus Receptus* version of the Greek New Testament. This text is the basis of the King James Version of the Scriptures. Some New Testament scholars, however, do not believe these verses were a part of Mark's gospel originally, but were added later and therefore were not part of the inspired canon of Scripture. If that is the case, the passage is not problematic with respect to the issue at hand.

It is beyond our purpose here to debate the issue of the *Textus Receptus* text versus the older texts upon which many modern translations are based. Even if we grant the validity of the passages in question, it can be easily harmonized with those which do not include baptism as a condition for salvation. This is done by taking seriously the concluding summary statement in verse 16. Here, lack of baptism is not included as a basis for condemnation but only disbelief: "he that believeth not shall be damned."

John 3:3-5 states:

> Jesus answered and said unto him, Verily, verily, I say unto thee, Except a man be born again, he cannot see the kingdom of God. Nicodemus saith unto Him, How can a man be born when he is old? can he enter the second time into his mother's womb, and be born? Jesus answered, Verily, verily, I say unto thee, Except a man be born of water and *of* the Spirit, he cannot enter into the kingdom of God.

Those who believe in baptismal regeneration frequently come to this passage for support.

Jack Cottrell argues,

> Given the probability that "water" in John 3:5 refers to Christian baptism and given the fact that "born again" and "kingdom of God" refer to salvation, we cannot avoid the conclusion that baptism is inseparable from the new birth and thus is a condition for salvation. This is in full agreement with the teaching of Mark 16:16.[42]

Contextually, it is much better to take the *water* in the passage to refer to the water or amniotic fluid which surrounds the fetus in the womb. After all, Nicodemus did make it plain by his question that he was thinking about physical birth (v. 4). The response Jesus gave him shows that this

---

42 Jack Cottrell, *Baptism, A Biblical Study* (Joplin, MO: College Press Publishing, 1989), pp. 45-46, 53, 60.

is precisely how Jesus understood him (v. 6). *Water* also sometimes refers symbolically to the Holy Spirit (cf. John 7:37-39) which is another valid interpretation not referring to water baptism.

One objection to this belief is often that in the amniotic fluid explanation, Jesus is saying the obvious—of course one has to be born the first time before he can be born the second time from above. At first this sounds like a valid objection. But do not we have something similar in John 11:26? There Jesus said to Martha, "Whosoever liveth and believeth in me shall never die." Did not the Savior know that no one could believe in Him who did not first live?

Acts 2:38-39 records the message of the Apostle Peter:

> Then Peter said unto them, Repent, and be baptized every one of you in the name of Jesus Christ for the remission of sins, and ye shall receive the gift of the Holy Ghost. For the promise is unto you, and to your children, and to all that are afar off, *even* as many as the Lord our God shall call.

Some say that this verse states clearly that baptism is the focal point of God's promises of forgiveness and the gift of the Holy Spirit. For example, Cottrell states,

> The conditions for receiving "double cure" according to Acts 2:38 are repentance and baptism, plus an implied faith . . . part of what a sinner must do to bring about forgiveness of his sins is to be baptized.[43]

I reject the view that water baptism is essential for salvation. There are alternative ways of understanding this verse which harmonize it with the rest of Scripture. It has been suggested that the word "believing" should be supplied, in keeping with the context. This would make the verse read "Repent, and be baptized every one of you [believing] in the name of Jesus Christ for the remission of sins."

---

43 Ibid., pp. 40, 41.

An even better solution is found in the text itself. The phrase translated "for the remission of sins" can mean "because of" or "for the purpose of" the remission of sins (cf. Matt. 12:41, where the same construction appears). Grammatically, it could be either. Since the consistent testimony of Scripture makes faith the only condition for salvation, and since there are Biblical examples where baptism was not performed for salvation (i.e., the thief on the cross), it seems best to translate the phrase as "because of the remission" here. In this way, the interpreter is true to the text and is in harmony with the rest of Scripture.

Acts 22:16 records this question given to Paul from Ananias:

> And now why tarriest thou? arise, and be baptized, and wash away thy sins, calling on the name of the Lord.

Cottrell speaks for those who believe in baptismal regeneration when he makes this comment:

> Thus Ananias's instruction does no less than confirm the obvious, a biblical testimony to the saving significance of baptism. God has promised to save us–to give us forgiveness of sins and the gift of the Holy Spirit–in Christian baptism.[44]

Ryrie has summarized the opposing view. His interpretation is exegetically sound and harmonizes this passage with those which make faith the sole condition for salvation:

> The verse contains four segments: (a) arise (which is a participle arising), (b) be baptized (an imperative), (c) wash away your sins (another imperative), and (d) calling on the name of the Lord (another participle). To make the verse teach baptism as necessary for salvation necessitates connecting parts 2 and 3—be baptized and wash away. But rather than being connected to each other, each of those two commands is actually connected with a participle. Arising is necessary be-

---

44 Ibid., p. 75.

fore baptism, and calling before sins can be washed away. Thus the verse should be read this way: arising, be baptized; wash away your sins, calling on the Lord. The verse correctly understood does not teach baptismal regeneration.[45]

Repentance. Usually those who see water baptism as a condition for salvation in addition to faith see repentance in the same way. Some feel including repentance in addition to faith in the gospel serves to reduce the number of *easy believism* converts. *Easy believism* refers to those who *accept Christ* but whose lives reveal no commitment, fruit or obedience to Christ.

Many have read into the meaning of the word *repentance* the idea of sorrow and have thereby implied that sorrow for sin is the same as repentance for sin. There is no doubt that genuine repentance will be accompanied by sorrow, but it is also true that one can be sorrowful without repenting.

The word *repentance* means *a change of mind.* Because of the confusion described above, many make repentance a *separate and additional* condition of salvation. This is not true in the Word. There is no question about it; repentance is necessary for salvation. However, Scripture views repentance as included in believing and not as an additional and separate condition to faith. All who have trusted Christ as Savior have changed their minds regarding Him and their sin. (Of course, it would be impossible to change one's mind without trusting the Savior.[46])

According to Scriptural usage, repentance is almost a synonym for faith.[47] Paul said he testified "both to the Jews, and also to the Greeks, repentance toward God, and faith toward our Lord Jesus Christ" (Acts 20:21; cf. 11:21).

---

45 Charles C. Ryrie, *Basic Theology* (Wheaton, IL: Victor Books, 1986), p. 337.

46 Zane C. Hodges, *Absolutely Free* (Grand Rapids: Zondervan Publishing Co., 1989) pp. 167-80. Hodges does not see repentance as the other side of the same coin as faith. Rather, he sees it as one of several ways God uses to prepare the sinner to accept the Savior's free gift of salvation.

47 For a definitive work on the relation of faith to repentance concluding with the view expressed above, see Robert Nichols Wilkin, *Repentance as a Condition for Salvation in the New Testament* (unpublished ThD dissertation, Dallas Theological Seminary, 1985).

God the Holy Spirit uses the facts of Scripture and causes the sinner to change his mind about himself, his sin, and the Savior. At the same time the Holy Spirit shows him his need of trusting Christ for salvation. In repentance, the sinner turns from himself and his sin. In faith, the sinner turns to the Savior for salvation.

Public confession. Some people say that a public confession of Christ is necessary for salvation.

Romans 10:9-10 is used to support this view:

> That if thou shalt confess with thy mouth the Lord Jesus, and shalt believe in thine heart that God hath raised him from the dead, thou shalt be saved. For with the heart man believeth unto righteousness; and with the mouth confession is made unto salvation.

But nothing about public confession is included in the verses. The confession referred to could just as well be a private confession to God. This has to do with one's open acknowledgement of his need and Christ's salvation. To confess Christ to others is part of the normal Christian experience, the result of new life within. One who has received Christ will usually want to make his faith known to others. But this is not a requirement for salvation. Rather, the sinner makes the confession because he has salvation.

If public confession is in view here as a condition of salvation, what about the many who have been saved under circumstances which made a public testimony impossible (i.e., what about the deaf and dumb or deathbed conversions)? The condition of salvation must be the same for all who can meet it. Note also how verse 10 clarifies the whole matter. It is through faith alone that the sinner is declared righteous. Confession is not *for* salvation but is *because* of it.

Jesus and others in the New Testament constantly invited others to accept Him and the salvation He offered. It seems just as valid to make the invitation in a church service as in private. The confession in either case, however, is not what brings salvation. Christ does, since He alone is the Savior of sinners.

Prayer. Sincere Christians often tell the unsaved to beg God for mercy. Appeal is frequently made to Luke 18:13 and the prayer of the publican, "God be merciful to me a sinner." But this prayer was prayed before the accomplishments of Calvary were a reality in time. The publican asked God to provide satisfaction for his sin. God has done just that in the person of Jesus Christ. In fact, God can be no more merciful than He has been at the cross. The work is finished. All that remains now is for man to believe. How simple. Salvation is free to the sinner—absolutely free.

Prayer must never be viewed as a condition for salvation. The newborn child of God will no doubt express his faith in prayer. Prayer does not save, however. Multitudes of people *pray* who are not saved. Scripture does not condition salvation upon prayer. Prayer is for the child of God. It is his means of communing with his heavenly Father. The calling in Romans 10:13 need not be understood as an audible prayer. Rather, in context, it refers to the *call* or cry of the heart to God in faith.

Isaiah 55:6 is sometimes used to stress the need of seeking the Lord for salvation. This was said not to the church, but to the nation of Israel and meant that they, as God's chosen people, were to return to Him. The New Testament reveals that Christ came "to seek and to save that which was lost" (Luke 19:10).

The unsaved are often told to confess their sin to be saved, and John's exhortation in 1 John 1:9 is used for Scriptural support. However, this text relates to Christians only. The unsaved are never told to confess their sins to be saved. They are called only to believe on the Lord Jesus Christ, and God says they will be saved (Acts 16:31; John 3:18).

WHAT HAVE WE DISCOVERED?

—◆◆◆—

I felt burdened to write this book. It stemmed from the reality that some who claimed to be evangelical were making known that they did not believe in the eternal punishment of those destined for hell. I was really shocked and stunned when I became aware that within the evangelical fold there was such denial of what the Bible clearly teaches about hell.

In Part 1, we first dealt with what Scripture teaches about heaven and its reality. We discussed who goes there after death, who cannot go to heaven, what we will do in heaven and the blessed hope that believers have of spending eternity in heaven.

In Part 2, we discovered what God's Word tells us about hell. We concentrated on the four views of hell held by *evangelicals*. We discovered that there are four different views of how hell is viewed today. The titles of those views are the literal view by Dr. John Walvoord, the metaphorical view by William Crockett, the purgatorial view held by Zachary Hayes, and the conditional view held by Clark Pinnock.

There is no doubt about it! We live in a troubled world today. Things are changing so fast that it is hard to remain current. There have always been different views about a lot of things. Some changes have been made in many areas. Some of the changes were and still are good, and others are not good. Think for a moment of all the changes in how we wash our clothes or how we go every place we want to. We fly anywhere in the world we want to. We do not live by the light of candles today. We have medical means for just almost everything that ails us. The list could go on and on.

However, when we think about where we will spend eternity, it matters mighty much, don't you think? God's Word has much to say about where each of us will spend eternity.

Helen Mirrenin, a 70-year-old acting star said recently, "But you only have two   options in life: die young or get old. There is nothing else."

You are wrong, Helen, there is something else. You, and all of us, must decide where we will spend eternity.

That decision is up to us in the sovereign plan of God. Do not forget that no one will go to heaven because he or she believes there is a God or tries hard to live a good honest life, or gives to the poor and needy, or goes to church a lot, or even reads the Bible a lot. The Bible makes it very clear that:

> God so loved the world that He gave His only begotten Son, that whosoever believeth in Him should not perish, but have everlasting life (John 3:16).

Furthermore, it says,

> For by grace are ye saved through faith; and that not of yourselves: *it is* the gift of God: Not of works, lest any man should boast (Eph. 2:8-9).

Jesus Christ paid the penalty for our sin. So, the decision is up to us to either accept Him as our sin-bearer and go to heaven when we die or reject the gift of God and spend eternity in hell.

We raised a question in Part 3. What about suicide? The Bible does record that some people did take their own lives. Several passages of Scripture were given in support of this. There does not seem to be any Scripture which clearly condemns suicide or condones it. It does certainly teach us to live our lives as believers for God's honor and glory. Unbelievers are also encouraged in the Bible to accept Christ as their personal Savior and to respect the lives of others. Never in the Bible is suicide encouraged or presented as a viable solution to one's problems.

In Part 4, we discussed God's future judgments: the future judgment seat of Christ for believers, the great white throne judgment for unbelievers, and judgments of Satan and the wicked angels.

I raised a question in Part 5: Where will you spend eternity? I truly trust that you will think seriously about that question before you do anything else.

Surely, you want to go to heaven. I have never heard about someone wanting to go to hell. Christ died for all mankind. His death on the cross paid for our sin. To be sure of heaven you must accept Christ as your Savior, the One who was your substitute on the cross of Calvary.

BIBLIOGRAPHY

Berkhof, Louis. *Systematic Theology*. Grand Rapids: Eerdmans, 1941.

_____. Systematic Theology. Grand Rapids: Eerdmans, 1968.

Blanchard, John. *Whatever Happened to Hell?* Durham, DL1 1RQ, England: Evangelical Press, 1993.

Buis, Harry. *The Doctrine of Eternal Punishment*. Philadelphia: Presbyterian and Reformed Publishing Co., 1957.

Burnham, Sophy. *Reflections on Angels, Past and Present and True Stories of How They Touched Our Lives*. New York: Ballantine, 1990.

Buswell, James Oliver. *A Systematic Theology of the Christian Religion*. Grand Rapids: Zondervan, 1971.

Chafer, Lewis Sperry. *Salvation*. Wheaton, IL: Van Kampen Press, 1917.

Clemons, James T. *What Does the Bible Say About Suicide?* Minneapolis: Fortress Press, 1990.

Cottrell, Jack. *Baptism*. Joplin, MO: College Press Publishing Co., 1989.

Couch, Mal and Lacy. *Going Home*. Springfield, MO: 21st Century Press, 2006.

Date, Christopher M. and Highfield, Ron. *A Consuming Passion*. Eugene, OR: Pickwick Publications, Wipf & Stock, 2015.

Davidson, Gustav. *A Dictionary of Angels*. New York: Free, 1967

Dickason, C. Fred. *Angels Elect and Evil*. Chicago: Moody Press, 1975

Gooder, Paula. *Heaven*. Eugene, OR: Cascade Books, 2011.

Gromacki, Robert G. *Are These the Last Days?* Old Tappan, NJ: Fleming H. Revell Co., 1970.

Hodge, Charles. *Systematic Theology*. Grand Rapids: Eerdmans, 1968.

Hodges, Zane C. *Absolutely Free*. Grand Rapids: Zondervan, 1989.

Kvanvig, Jonatehan L. *The Problem of Hell*. New York: Oxford University Press, 1993.

Lahaye, Tim and Hindson, Ed., Eds. *The Popular Encyclopedia of Bible Prophecy*. Eugene, OR: Harvest House Publishers, 2004.

Laney, J. Carl. *Answers to Tough Questions*. Grand Rapids: Kregel, 1997.

Lightner, Robert P. *Angels, Satan, and Demons*. Plano, TX: IFL Publishing House, Divison of Insight for Living, 2010.

_____. *The Death Christ Died*. Grand Rapids: Kregel, 1998.

_____. *Handbook of Evangelical Theology*. Grand Rapids: Kregel, 1995.

_____. *Heaven for Those Who Can't Believe.* Schaumburg, IL: Regular Baptist Press, 1997.

_____. *Last Days Handbook.* Eugene, OR: Wipf & Stock, 1997.

_____. *Sin, the Savior, and Salvation.* Grand Rapids: Kregel, 1991.

_____. *Speaking in Tongues and Divine Healing.* Schaumburg, IL: Regular Baptist Press, 1978.

Lockyer, Herbert. *All the Angels in the Bible.* Peabody, MA: Hendrickson, 1996.

Machen, J. Gresham. *What Is Faith?* Grand Rapids: Eerdmans, 1925.

Meeter, John, ed. *Selected Shorter Writings of Benjamin B. Warfield.* Nutley, NJ: Presbyterian and Reformed Publishing Co., 1970.

Morgan, Christopher W. and Peterson, Robert A., general eds. *Heaven.* Wheaton, IL: Crossway, 2014.

_____. *Hell Under Fire.* Grand Rapids: Zondervan, 2004.

Oatman, Johnson, Jr. and Sweney, John R. *Sing Men Number Two.* Wheaton: IL: Singspiration, 1950. Used by permission.

Packer, J. I. *Fundamentalism and the Word of God.* Grand Rapids: Eerdmans, 1960.

_____. *Knowing God.* Downers Grove, IL: InterVarsity Press, 1973.

Pentecost, J. Dwight. *Things To Come.* Grand Rapids: Zondervan, 1958.

Peterson, Robert A. *Hell on Trial: The Case for Eternal Punishment.* Phillipsburg, NJ: P&R Publishing, 1995.

Pinnock, Clark H., gen. ed. *The Grace of God, the Will of Man.* Grand Rapids: Zondervan, 1989.

Ryrie, Charles Caldwell. *Basic Theology.* Wheaton, IL: Victor Books, 1986.

_____. *Dispensationalism Today.* Chicago, IL: Moody Press, 1965.

_____. *The Holy Spirit.* Chicago, IL: Moody Press, 1965.

_____. *Ryrie Study Bible Expanded Edition, New American Standard Bible.* Chicago: Moody Bible Institute, 1995.

Thayer, Joseph Henry. *Greek-English Lexicon of the New Testament.* Findlay, OH: Dunham Publishing Co., 1940.

Thiessen, Henry Clarence. *Introductory Lectures in Systematic Theology.* Grand Rapids: Eerdmans, 1949.

Toon, Peter. *Heaven and Hell.* Nashville, TN: Nelson Publishers, 1986.

Trickey-Bapty, Carolyn. *The Book of Angels.* Ambler, PA: Ottenheimer, 1994.

Walvoord, John F., Crockett, William, Hayes, Zachary, and Pinnock, Clark. William Crockett, ed. *Four Views on Hell.* Grand Rapids: Zondervan, 1992.

Webb, R. A. *The Theology of Infant Salvation.* Clarksville, TN: Presbyterian Committee of Publication, 1907.

Wilkin, Robert Nichols. *Repentance as a Condition for Salvation in the New Testament.* Unpublished THD dissertation, Dallas Theological Seminary, 1985.

Zuck, Roy B. *Precious in His Sight: Childhood and Children in the Bible.* Grand Rapids: Baker, 1996.

Dispensational Publishing House is striving to become the go-to source for Bible-based materials from the dispensational perspective.

Our goal is to provide high-quality doctrinal and worldview resources that make dispensational theology accessible to people at all levels of understanding.

Visit our blog regularly to read informative articles from both known and new writers.

And please let us know how we can better serve you.

Dispensational Publishing House, Inc.
PO Box 3181
Taos, NM 87571

Call us toll free 844-321-4202

CPSIA information can be obtained
at www.ICGtesting.com
Printed in the USA
FSHW01n2229060618
48918FS